PRESCRIPTION
AND OVER-THE-COUNTER DRUGS

BY VALERIE BODDEN

CONTENT CONSULTANT

SARAH T. MELTON, PHARMD, BCPP, BCACP, FASCP

PROFESSOR OF PHARMACY PRACTICE
GATTON COLLEGE OF PHARMACY AT EAST TENNESSEE STATE UNIVERSITY

Essential Library

An Imprint of Abdo Publishing | abdopublishing.com

ABDOPUBLISHING.COM

Published by Abdo Publishing, a division of ABDO, PO Box 398166, Minneapolis, Minnesota 55439.
Copyright © 2019 by Abdo Consulting Group, Inc. International copyrights reserved in all countries.
No part of this book may be reproduced in any form without written permission from the publisher.
Essential Library™ is a trademark and logo of Abdo Publishing.

Printed in the United States of America, North Mankato, Minnesota
042018
092018

THIS BOOK CONTAINS
RECYCLED MATERIALS

Cover Photo: Sascha Burkard/Shutterstock Images
Interior Photos: Marc Bruxelle/Shutterstock Images, 4–5; Donald Gruener/iStockphoto, 8, 51; Soru
Epotok/Shutterstock Images, 10; Tony Hicks/AP Images, 13; Brooks/Brown/Science Source, 15;
NLM/Science Source, 18; Spencer Sutton/Science Source, 23; Darwin Brandis/iStockphoto, 24–25;
Red Line Editorial, 28, 41, 93; iStockphoto, 30, 85, 95; Jim Beckel/The Oklahoman/AP Images, 33;
Shutterstock Images, 34–35, 65, 76; Toby Talbot/AP Images, 39; Chris Gallagher/Science Source,
44–45; People Images/iStockphoto, 47; NY Daily News Archive/New York Daily News/Getty Images,
53; BSIP/Universal Images Group/Getty Images, 57; Tero Vesalainen/Shutterstock Images, 59; Steven
Senne/AP Images, 61; Craig Mitchelldyer/Getty Images News/Getty Images, 69; ESB Professional/
Shutterstock Images, 71; Katarzyna Bialasiewicz/iStockphoto, 79; Lynne Sladky/AP Images, 80–81;
Olivier Douliery/Abaca Press/Sipa/AP Images, 88–89; Spencer Platt/Getty Images News/Getty
Images, 99

Editor: Susan E. Hamen
Series Designer: Laura Polzin

Library of Congress Control Number: 2017961355

Publisher's Cataloging-in-Publication Data
Names: Bodden, Valerie, author.
Title: Prescription and over-the-counter drugs / by Valerie Bodden.
Description: Minneapolis, Minnesota : Abdo Publishing, 2019. | Series: Drugs in real life | Includes
        online resources and index.
Identifiers: ISBN 9781532114199 (lib.bdg.) | ISBN 9781532154027 (ebook)
Subjects: LCSH: Medication abuse--Juvenile literature. | Drug abuse--Social aspects--United States-
        -Juvenile literature. | Recreational drug use--Juvenile literature. | Drug control--United
        States--Juvenile literature.
Classification: DDC 362.299--dc23

CONTENTS

A NATIONAL EPIDEMIC

It was called the Graveyard of Overdoses. In a single 90-foot (27 m) stretch, one cemetery in Staten Island, New York, included the graves of 11 people between the ages of 20 and 41. All had died of drug overdoses within an 18-month period from 2014 to 2016. Prescription medications were a contributing factor in the deaths of at least six. These victims represent only a fraction of the more than 50,000 people who die of drug overdoses every year. While many overdose deaths can be attributed to illicit, or illegal, drugs such as heroin, prescription drugs accounted for more than one-half of all US drug overdose deaths

in 2015.[1] Among the young people buried in the Graveyard of Overdoses is Freddy Carrasco. In his early twenties, Freddy was in a serious car accident that injured his back. His doctor prescribed the painkiller oxycodone. Freddy was supposed to take one 20-milligram tablet six times a day. But soon, that wasn't enough. Freddy felt like he needed more. When his doctor refused to give him another prescription, Freddy started going to multiple doctors, convincing each to write him prescriptions for pain medications. Soon, Freddy lost interest in his favorite activities. His college grades began to slip. He began to steal money and jewelry from his parents in order to pay for his drug habit. Three times, Freddy sought treatment. But each time, he relapsed. When oxycodone wasn't enough, he started using heroin, a very potent opioid, as well. In May

LIVES TRANSFORMED

The lives of those who become addicted to prescription medication can become drastically affected. In an interview for a video about prescription drug abuse, former substance misuser Ed recounted the toll his addiction took on his life. "I've been using one drug or another since I was 14. Basically, the last 20 years, I've been in a coma. My direction in life was clouded continually by the use of mostly prescription medications—opiates, OxyContin, Oxycodone, sedatives, Valium, Xanax. . . . I've held jobs, but I've also lost jobs. I've lost friends."[2]

According to a 2014 survey, approximately 25 percent of all American teenagers misuse prescription drugs before graduating from high school.[3]

2015, Freddy's parents found him unresponsive in his room. He had died from a combination of oxycodone, methadone, and heroin.

Stories like Freddy's aren't confined to the Graveyard of Overdoses. They are repeated in communities around the country. Laura Hope Laws had been playing on the varsity soccer team since her freshman year of high school in Atlanta, Georgia. But after breaking her jaw in a game her freshman year, Laura was prescribed prescription painkillers. The painkillers didn't only ease Laura's pain. They made her feel good. When her prescription ran out, Laura needed a new source of medication. She stole prescription painkillers from her family's medicine cabinet. When that supply was no longer available, Laura started using a substance that was easier to get: heroin. Soon, Laura knew she needed help. She checked into a treatment program. By Thanksgiving of her senior year in high school, she was doing well. Her family planned to

YOUNGEST VICTIMS

Some of the youngest victims of the prescription drug misuse epidemic are toddlers who have stumbled upon prescription drugs and eaten them as if they were candy. In 2015, 87 young children died after accidentally ingesting opioid drugs.[4] "There are no pill parties happening in preschools," said Jennifer Plumb, an emergency room doctor. "These kids aren't making a choice because they are trying to get high on a substance. It's that the pills are everywhere."[5]

celebrate the holiday in Florida. But the night before they were scheduled to leave, Laura ran into an old friend. The friend gave her prescription morphine, along with alcohol and cocaine. The combination proved lethal. Laura was only 17 when she died.

Opioids are not the only prescription drugs with devastating effects. Kate Miller's first encounter with misusing prescription drugs occurred during her senior year of college at the University of California, Los Angeles. She had put off studying for finals and needed to cram. So, she bought some of the stimulant medication Adderall from a fellow student. Kate found that when she took Adderall, she could concentrate for hours at a time. When she moved to New York and got her first high-pressure job as a paralegal, she continued to take the drug. To make it easier

Some teens will look for prescription medications, including opioids, in their families' medicine cabinets.

to get the medication, she visited a doctor and told him she had attention deficit hyperactivity disorder (ADHD). The doctor gave her a prescription for Adderall. Soon, she took the medication not only to get through the workday, but also to give her the energy for wild nights of socializing. As she continued to take the drug, she found she needed more and more tablets to get the same effect. Soon, she was taking several a day.

Kate had always been careful not to drink too much in college because she knew her family had a history of alcoholism. But she convinced herself that her dependence on pills was different. "Because my drugs came from a doctor's [prescription pad] in an office … I felt safe," she said.[6]

Many people falsely believe prescription drugs are always safe because they are prescribed by a doctor.

WHAT ARE PRESCRIPTION DRUGS?

A drug is any chemical substance used to treat, cure, prevent, or diagnose a disease. Drugs cause changes in a person's mind, body, or both. Drugs can either help or harm the body. In fact, the same drug can be both beneficial and dangerous, depending on the dosage. As the Swiss physician Paracelsus said in the 1500s, "All substances are poisons; there is none which is not a poison. The right dose differentiates a poison and a remedy."[7]

Because of their potential to cause harm if misused, some medications are regulated by the federal government. These drugs are known as prescription drugs, or pharmaceuticals, because they can only be obtained with a prescription. Doctors, nurse practitioners, and physician's assistants can give patients prescriptions. The prescription includes instructions on how much of a drug to take and how often to take it. In determining which drugs to prescribe, health-care providers must consider adverse effects and weigh the risks and benefits of a specific drug for each individual.

PRESCRIPTION DRUG MISUSE

Prescription drug misuse occurs whenever someone uses a drug that was not prescribed for him or her. This includes using a prescription medicine shared by a friend or family member. Prescription drug misuse also occurs when people take more of their own medication than the doctor prescribed or alter the drug's form, such as by crushing it in order to snort or inject it. Taking prescription drugs to get high is another form of prescription drug misuse.

Taking a prescription prescribed for another person is illegal. It is also dangerous. It can lead to dependence, substance

THE GOOD AND THE BAD

There is a common misconception that only illegal drugs are harmful if taken. However, even prescription drugs can be fatal if taken incorrectly. "We can label drugs as being 'good' or 'bad,' medicinal or illicit," explains Nicole Kweik, Director of Undergraduate Studies at Ohio State University College of Pharmacy. "However, the body doesn't care about the name of the drug or from where the drug came. The body, and more specifically the targets (of a drug), react according to the chemistry of the drugs."[8]

use disorder, and often death. Substance use disorder, sometimes referred to as addiction, occurs when a person begins using a substance on a regular basis despite the harm it can cause. In 2011, the Centers for Disease Control and Prevention (CDC), a federal agency that conducts and supports health promotion, declared prescription drug misuse a national epidemic. By 2017, the epidemic had become so widespread that the CDC reported American life expectancy had fallen for the first time in more than two decades. According to the CDC, the abuse of opioids—both prescription painkillers and illicit drugs such as heroin and fentanyl—had shaved two and a half months off average life expectancy.[9] The crisis had people across the nation scrambling to find solutions as drug deaths continued to rise.

FINANCIAL TIMES

WORLD BUSINESS NEWSPAPER

FRIDAY 22 APRIL 2016

UK £2.70 Channel Islands £3.00 Republic of Ireland €3.00

Europe's hostages
Ever-closer union or it's fingers in the post — ROBERT SHRIMSLEY, PAGE 10

How to spend it
A 38-page special edition on men's style — MAGAZINE

Gillian Tett
Dull bank returns are the new normal — COMMENT PAGE 11

Government open to Tata Steel stake

The government has said it is ready to buy an equity stake in Tata Steel's UK operation, the first time that a Conservative administration has contemplated such a part-nationalisation since before the Thatcher era.

Sajid Javid, business secretary, raised the prospect in a statement that also said the government is prepared to provide "hundreds of millions of pounds" in debt financing to back a rescue of the steel operations, including the Port Talbot plant in Wales.

A state stake would be limited to less than 25 per cent. "We are not seeking control of the company," a spokeswoman for the prime minister said.

Javid eyes equity stake page 4
Lombard page 20

End of purple reign Pop back in mourning as Prince dies

Superstar dies, page 5

VW moves to draw line under US ~~deal~~ with offer to buy back cars

Briefing

■ **SunEdison files for Chapter 11**
SunEdison, the world's largest renewable energy developer, has filed for bankruptcy protection, ending its bid to become a solar and wind power "vapormajor" — PAGE 15; FT BIG READ, PAGE 9

■ **Recorded killings reverse recent trend**
The number of recorded homicides in England and Wales rose 11 per cent in the year to December, suggesting that a decade-long downward trend may be coming to an end. — PAGE 4

■ **Mitsubishi's R&D centre raided**
Regulators have raided Mitsubishi Motors' R&D centre after the group admitted to falsifying fuel economy data. Investors have had to digest news of the fraud, which some analysts have said could cost the carmaker nearly $900m. — PAGE 16

■ **Lloyds retrenches as TSB surges**
Lloyds is to cut more than 600 jobs and close 21 branches amid its major shake-up plan. Meanwhile, TSB, carved out of Lloyds in 2013, posted a 55 per cent surge in quarterly profits. — PAGE 19/GB, PAGE 16

■ **Brussels toughens tax crackdown**
The EU commissioner in charge of corporate transparency said it was unacceptable that the wealthy could hide money abroad to avoid paying tax. — PAGE 6; EDITORIAL COMMENT, PAGE 10

■ **Ecuador 'earthquake tax' promised**
Ecuador's president has pledged a wealth tax on the country's millionaires to help raise the billions of dollars needed to rebuild the country, which was recently hit by a devastating earthquake. — PAGE 9

■ **Blackstone quarterly profits fall 77%**
Blackstone, the world's biggest asset manager, suffered from sharply lower performance fees amid turbulent markets in the first three months of the year. Profits fell 77 per cent. — PAGE 18/US, PAGE 16

THE Sun

Friday, April 22, 2016 · BRITAIN'S BEST-SELLING PAPER · 50p · thesun.co.uk

UK DIESEL CARS RAP
By CRAIG WOODHOUSE
BRITAIN'S favourite diesel cars belch out up to 12 times the legal pollution limit on roads after being tuned to beat tests in labs, an investigation reveals.
Full Story — Page Six

FREE Panini
Euro 2016 stickers
VOUCHER SEE PAGE 30

PRINCE DIES ON QUEEN'S BIRTHDAY

By DAN WOOTTON, Associate Editor

MUSIC icon Prince was yesterday found dead in a lift aged 57 — sparking shock across the world.

The body of the seven-time Grammy winner, behind generation-defining hits such as Purple Rain and 1999, was discovered at his Minnesota compound at 3.45pm UK time.

Cops said they were called to an "unresponsive adult male" but life-saving attempts failed. His death, on the day of the Queen's 90th, followed reports the singer had a severe bout of flu. Last night it was claimed he may have had pneumonia.

PURPLE REIGN IS OVER
LEGEND, 57, FOUND SLUMPED IN LIFT

SEE PAGES 2, 3, 4 & 5

Friday April 22, 2016 | thetimes.co.uk | No 71891

Brexit effect on house price
Bricks & Mortar

~~Students~~ dump student union

ende on severing ties with the NUS and said that it was in touch with students planning disaffiliation campaigns at the universities of Durham, Edinburgh, York, Westminster, Aberystwyth and London South Bank, as well as at the London School of Economics and King's College London.

A mass withdrawal from membership would be a severe blow to the NUS...

Prince in his pomp in 1985. He sold more than 100 million records...

CHAPTER TWO

USE AND ABUSE

The history of drug use dates back more than 6,000 years. People in ancient Mesopotamia made use of the milky white fluid produced by bulbs of the opium poppy. The fluid was dried into a sticky substance known today as opium. The earliest recorded prescription is a Sumerian clay tablet dating to around 2250 BCE. The prescription recognized the pain-killing and sedative qualities of opium. An Egyptian papyrus from 1552 BCE described the use of opium to create more than 700 different medications.

Other early prescriptions described the use of hundreds of other plants and minerals. Among the most common were pine turpentine, the aromatic root calamus, flowering plants cannabis and crocus, and castor, which is an oil obtained from the glands of beavers. In China, leaves and branches of the ephedra plant

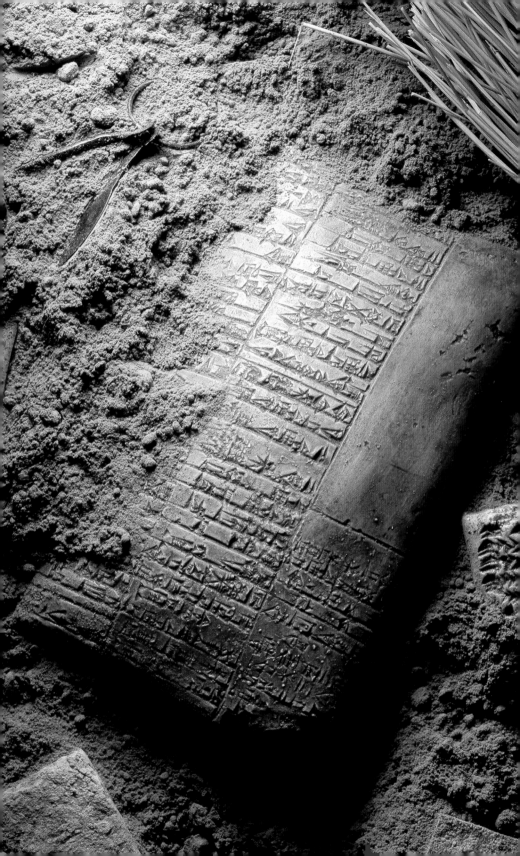

Turkish and Arab traders first brought opium to China in the 700s. At first, opium was restricted to medicinal uses. But by the 1700s, recreational opium use, or use for the purpose of pleasure instead of medical reasons, had become widespread. This led the Chinese government to ban its use in 1799. Foreign nations were banned from trading opium in China. But British merchants who had become wealthy off the opium trade continued to ship opium into China. The Chinese seized 20,000 chests of British opium in March 1839.[2] This sparked the First Opium War between China and Britain. The war ended with British victory in 1842. As a result, China had to pay a large fine, surrender Hong Kong to the British, and allow for British trading in China.

The Second Opium War broke out in 1856 after Chinese officials boarded a British trading ship. The French joined with the British in fighting Chinese forces. British and French victory in 1860 led to widespread opium importation into China. By 1900, one-quarter of China's population was addicted to opium.[3]

were used to treat headaches and colds.

NEW MEDICINES

In 1524, Swiss physician Paracelsus returned to Europe from a trip to Egypt and Arabia. While there, he had been introduced to a tincture of opium. Paracelsus called the new drug laudanum, from the Latin word meaning "to be praised."[1] It was used to treat everything from colds and flu to insomnia and fussiness in babies. Soon, laudanum was being taken not only by those with legitimate health concerns but also by those who simply wanted to feel good or leave their worries behind.

Laudanum remained the opiate of choice until 1803, when German chemist Friedrich Sertürner isolated the active ingredient in opium—morphine.

Named for Morpheus, the Greek god of dreams, morphine was ten times more potent than raw opium. In 1832, codeine was separated from opium. This substance was less potent than morphine. Both drugs were soon available in the United States and elsewhere without a prescription. Morphine use took off during the Civil War (1861–1865), when it was given to soldiers wounded on the battlefield. By the end of the war, an estimated 400,000 men were addicted to the drug.[4]

A growing number of women became addicted to morphine and other opium products as well, largely because of how common the use of patent medicines had become. Manufacturers claimed these drugs cured everything from fevers and colds to arthritis and depression. Manufacturers did not have to reveal the contents

The word "pill" comes from the Latin word *pillula,* meaning "little ball," because people used to mash drugs into a ball of bread or clay to make them easier to swallow.

UNDERSTANDING MISUSE

Part of effectively dealing with the prescription drug misuse epidemic is understanding the reasons why it has become so prevalent. In an interview, clinical psychologist B. Christopher Frueh stated one of the reasons he believes prescription medication misuse has increased, explaining,

> I think we've become a society that has very low distress tolerance. Somebody has a symptom, we need to find a quick fix for it. Somebody is uncomfortable, we rush in with all kinds of ways of changing things for them. . . . Somebody's having symptoms, we have a medication.[5]

of their patent medicines to consumers. They were sold by stores, traveling salesmen, and mail order without regulation. Some, such as Mrs. Winslow's Soothing Syrup, were intended for children. The most common ingredients in these medications were alcohol, opium and opium derivatives, and cocaine.

THE FIRST DRUG PROBLEM

With patent medicine sales soaring, drug overdose deaths became common, especially among children. By 1900, an estimated 250,000 Americans—or 1 of every 300 people—were addicted to opium.[6] Most of those addicted were middle-class women who had used patent medicines.

By 1868, 1.5 million bottles of Mrs. Winslow's Soothing Syrup were sold annually. They were administered primarily to children.

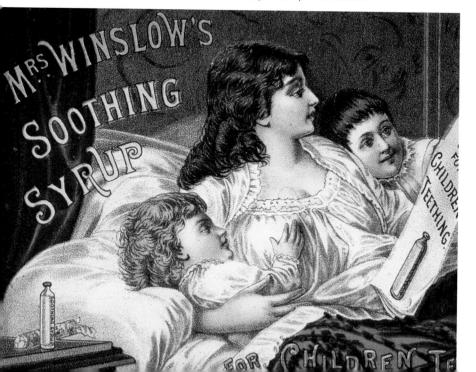

The first federal drug law was aimed not at reducing drug use but at informing the public of the contents of patent medicines. The Pure Food and Drug Act of 1906 required that all patent medications include a label indicating their contents. It did not outlaw the use of any substance in these medications. In 1914, the Harrison Narcotic Act regulated the use of opium-containing products.

Other substances faced fewer regulations. During World War II (1939–1945), soldiers on both sides were issued large quantities of amphetamines. These drugs helped the men remain awake and alert during combat. After the war, these drugs were used by truckers, factory workers, and athletes to increase alertness and performance. Those who abused amphetamines by day might turn to barbiturates to help them sleep at night. Barbiturates are depressants and have a sedative effect.

WHAT'S IN A NAME?

The same drug can go by several names. A drug's chemical name describes its molecular structure. The chemical name for morphine, for example, is (5a,6a)-7,8-didehydro-4,5-epoxy-17-methylmorphinan-3,6-diol. The generic name of a drug is a simpler name it is commonly known by, such as the name *morphine*. A drug's trade name is the trademarked name under which a drug is sold by a specific manufacturer. Trade names for morphine include Kadian, MorphaBond, and MS Contin. Drugs taken for nonmedical purposes often also have street names. Street names for morphine include dreamer, mister blue, morph, and monkey.

TIGHTER REGULATION

As abuse of all these substances increased, the government worked to set stricter regulations on their use. These efforts resulted in the Controlled Substances Act of 1970. The act, which remains in effect today, places all drugs with the potential for abuse into one of five categories, or schedules. A drug's schedule is determined by its potential for misuse, its medical value, and its safety when used under the supervision of a doctor. Schedule I drugs have the highest potential for misuse and are considered to have no medicinal value. With the exception of marijuana in some states, these drugs cannot be used even with a prescription. Schedule I drugs include heroin, marijuana, LSD, and psilocybin. Schedule II drugs, such as morphine, cocaine, hydrocodone, and methamphetamine, have high potential for misuse but are used for some medical treatments. Schedule III drugs have less potential for misuse and are currently used in medical treatments. Codeine, anabolic

SHOOTING UP

The invention of the hypodermic needle in 1848 accelerated the pace of drug abuse. The needle allowed substances such as morphine to be directly injected into the bloodstream. Substances that provided a mild, long-lasting effect when ingested created a faster, more intense, shorter-lasting experience when injected, or shot up. The intense, short-lived high of injected drugs created an intense craving for more, causing addiction rates to skyrocket in the late 1800s. Hypodermic needles could be purchased at the nearest drugstore, and some women even wore syringes disguised as jewelry pinned to their clothing.

steroids, and some barbiturates fall into Schedule III. Schedule IV drugs, such as alprazolam and diazepam, have lower potential

for misuse and are used medically. Schedule V drugs have the lowest potential for misuse. They include some cough medications containing codeine. In 1973, the Drug Enforcement Administration (DEA) was created. It is the DEA's responsibility to enforce the Controlled Substances Act and regulate the use of controlled substances.

DRUGS OF ABUSE

Not all prescription drugs are abused. Drugs of abuse are generally psychoactive drugs—that is, drugs that affect the brain. They include opioids, stimulants, central nervous system depressants, and even some over-the-counter medications.

These drugs work on chemicals in the brain known as neurotransmitters. Neurotransmitters help send messages between the brain's 100 billion neurons, or nerve cells. Neurons are separated by tiny gaps called synapses. Neurotransmitters travel through these synapses to send messages from one neuron to another. The end of the neuron that receives the message is known as the receptor. The neurotransmitter attaches to the receptor like a key in a lock. Each kind of receptor can receive only specific neurotransmitters.

Opioids such as heroin cause the brain's neurons to release dopamine, represented here by the red pyramids. This release creates a rush of pleasure.

Some psychoactive drugs affect the brain's natural chemical communication by mimicking the effects of the body's own neurotransmitters. These drugs are able to attach to receptors, but their effects are often more powerful than those of the body's natural neurotransmitters. Other drugs can cause neurons to release too much of a specific neurotransmitter, such as dopamine. Dopamine is a neurotransmitter responsible for feelings of pleasure or euphoria.

A neuron can send and receive up to 400 signals a second.

CHAPTER THREE

DRUG CULTURE

Prescription drugs have been developed to treat everything from strep throat to diabetes to severe pain. Today, pharmaceuticals represent a multibillion-dollar industry. In 2014, patients in the United States filled more than 4.3 billion prescriptions.[1] About 300 million were for pain medications, making the United States the largest consumer of painkillers in the world. With about 5 percent of the world's population, the United States consumes 80 percent of the world's pain medications.[2] About 70 percent of Americans take at least one prescription medication each day, while more than one-half take two or more.[3]

Since 1999, the CDC has seen a steady climb in the number of Americans who use prescription medications.

▶

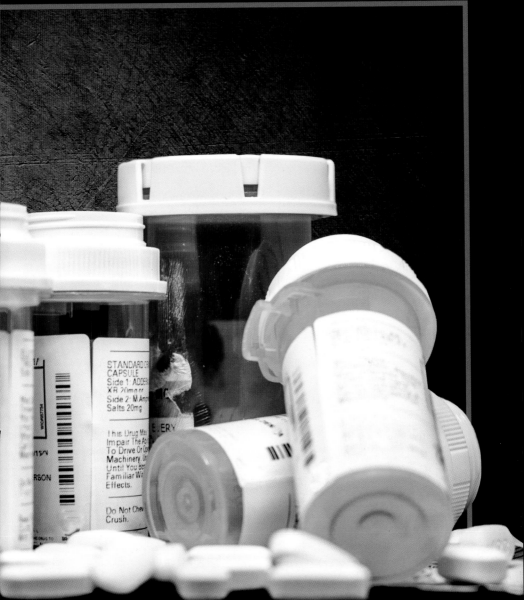

ARE DRUG COMPANIES TO BLAME?

In September 2017, the attorneys general from 41 states announced an investigation of the pharmaceutical companies responsible for manufacturing opioid pain relievers. Their action came as the pharmaceutical industry faced dozens of lawsuits from states, cities, and counties for its role in fueling the opioid crisis. In one lawsuit, Ohio attorney general Mike DeWine accused pharmaceutical companies of spending "millions of dollars on promotional activities and materials that falsely deny or trivialize the risks of opioids while overstating the benefits of using them for chronic pain."[6] The lawsuit seeks financial compensation for the rising costs of government-funded health insurance plans such as Medicaid, emergency response, and addiction treatment as a result of prescription opioid abuse.

Some legal experts believed the suits would be hard to win. Some felt that manufacturers would shift the blame to the prescribers or to the patients themselves for taking the drugs in ways other than prescribed.

Although they were developed to help people with health problems, prescription drugs have become some of the most misused substances. According to the National Survey on Drug Use and Health, an estimated 18.7 million Americans over the age of 12 misused prescription drugs at least once in 2016. That number represents 6.9 percent of the American population age 12 and older.[4] The only drug more widely abused was marijuana, which 13.9 percent of Americans age 12 and older reported using.[5] More people misused prescription drugs than used cocaine, methamphetamine, and heroin combined.

Opioid pain relievers are the most commonly abused prescription drugs. About 11.5 million people misused prescription opioids at least once in 2016.[7] About 3.3 million people were current misusers of these drugs, meaning they had misused prescription opioids in the past month. Another 2 million people misused prescription tranquilizers in the same period, while 1.7 million abused prescription stimulants, and 0.5 million misused prescription sedatives.[8] Overall prescription drug abuse declined slightly from 2015 but was matched by a simultaneous increase in the use of the illicit opioid heroin.

WHO ABUSES PRESCRIPTION DRUGS?

People of all ages and backgrounds misuse prescription drugs. "This epidemic, it's got no face," according to Chris Eisele, president of the Warren County Fire Chiefs' Association in Ohio, one of the states hardest hit by the opioid epidemic.[9] Prescription drugs are the third-most-common substance of abuse among young people, after alcohol and marijuana. According to the National Survey on Drug Use and Health, 5.3 percent of young people between the ages of 12 and 17 misused prescription drugs in 2016.[10] Abuse of prescription medications is even more common among young adults between the ages of 18 and 25, with 14.5 percent reporting misusing prescription drugs in 2016. Older adults are not immune, either. About 5.9 percent of adults age 26 or older misused prescription drugs in 2016.[11]

The prevalence of prescription drug abuse has led to an increase in the number of overdose deaths. Drug overdose has

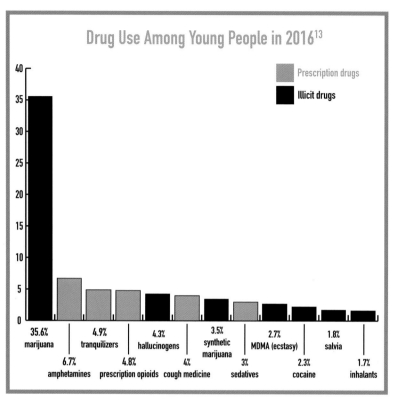

Prescription drugs

Illicit drugs

35.6% marijuana   4.9% tranquilizers   4.3% hallucinogens   3.5% synthetic marijuana   2.7% MDMA (ecstasy)   1.8% salvia

6.7% amphetamines   4.8% prescription opioids   4% cough medicine   3% sedatives   2.3% cocaine   1.7% inhalants

The bar graph above shows the percentage of twelfth grade students who misused specific drugs in 2016.

been the leading cause of accidental death in the United States since 2009, overtaking car accidents and gun deaths. In 2015, accidental overdoses killed 52,000 people. More than 22,000 of these deaths resulted from prescription opioid pain relievers, and 9,000 involved prescription depressants. Deaths from overdose increased in 2016 to 64,000, fueled largely by illicit opioids such as heroin and fentanyl.[12]

Approximately 175 people in the United States die every day as a result of drug overdose.[14]

REASONS FOR MISUSE

People misuse prescription drugs for a number of reasons. Of those who misused prescription pain relievers in 2016, more than 60 percent reported they used the drugs to relieve physical pain.[15] Others misuse prescription drugs to help them relax or deal with stress and anxiety. Some misuse prescription drugs to overcome feelings of depression or to help them sleep. People misuse prescription stimulants to increase their energy and improve performance at school, at work, or in sports.

While some people seek physical or mental benefits from abusing prescription drugs, others use the drugs simply to get high, or feel good. "I just like the feeling of certain things being high," Cory, an opioid misuser, said. "It wasn't like, 'I'm depressed so I'm going to take this to make me feel better.' It was kind of like, 'I'm feeling good, I'm gonna try this to see if I can feel

ILLEGAL TO USE OR DISTRIBUTE

Although prescription drugs are legal when used correctly, taking them without a prescription is just as illegal as taking illicit drugs. Distributing prescription drugs—either by selling them or simply giving them away—is also illegal. Possession or distribution of these substances without a prescription can lead to felony charges, large fines, and prison terms. Possession of certain drugs without a doctor's prescription can result in a $1,000 fine and a prison term of up to one year. Selling or giving away drugs is a more serious offense and can lead to a $2 million fine and five years in prison. Fines and prison terms increase for subsequent offenses.

Athletes can be at risk when a sports injury leads to misuse of prescription pain relievers.

even more better.'"[16] Other users may not be seeking a high but may take prescription drugs simply to experiment or because they feel pressured by their friends.

DRUGS EVERYWHERE

One reason people may be so willing to experiment with prescription drugs is they mistakenly believe prescription drugs are safer to use than street, or illegal, drugs. This is because they are prescribed by doctors, dispensed by pharmacies, and approved by the Food and Drug Administration (FDA). In a 2013 survey, nearly 25 percent of teens said misusing prescription drugs was not risky, while 16 percent of their parents believed misusing prescription drugs was safer than using illicit drugs.[17]

Some people blame the growing prescription drug abuse problem on the fact that prescription drugs are so prevalent in American culture. People take medications to deal with an array of medical and psychological issues. Additionally, new prescription medications are widely advertised. As a result, taking these drugs is seen as a normal part of everyday life. "It is difficult to live drug-free in a society flooded with quick-fix drug advertising. Sometimes, it seems almost un-American to endure aches and pains without doing something about them," said Nan Davis, founder of Pharmacy Counseling Services.[18]

The widespread use of prescription drugs means they are easy to get, even for people without a prescription. More than one-half of people who misuse prescription drugs obtain them from family or friends for free. People are often happy to share their extra medications with others experiencing similar symptoms, even though doing so is illegal. Others pay friends or family members for medications. Others simply take medications out of a friend's or family member's medicine cabinet without

JUST ONE PILL

Cory, a young man who became addicted to opiates at the age of 17, described how easily he became addicted after just one pill. Despite growing up in a very close and supportive family, he fell into prescription drug abuse. "You know the drugs . . . feel like they took my mind over and made me do things that (I was) brought up not to do, you know. And it just turned me into a monster."[19]

asking permission. "You know, I just went into my medicine cabinet, and my buddy is like, 'Oh, hey, these will get you high. Let's do some,'" said one prescription drug misuser. "So I was like, 'Okay, ya know, you talked me into it. They're right here. I don't have to pay anything. Sure.'"[20]

Others obtain the prescription medications they misuse from doctors. To convince a doctor to prescribe the medications, they may describe false symptoms. Or, they may shop for doctors, visiting multiple doctors to obtain a large quantity of prescription medications. Some people visit "pill mills," or clinics where unethical health-care workers write prescriptions for large quantities of medications or prescribe medications for those without a medical need. Others buy prescription medications from internet pharmacies that will ship medications without first receiving a doctor's prescription. People with an addiction to prescription drugs may resort to stealing them from clinics, hospitals, or pharmacies. Some steal

THE DOWNWARD SPIRAL OF ADDICTION

In an antidrug education video called "Chasing the Dragon: The Life of an Opiate Addict," former FBI director James Comey warns teens, "Those whose lives are taken over by drug addiction are often kids from stable homes with strong families—good people who had great childhoods, were given everything they wanted, and had everything going for them. But they took one wrong turn and they were hooked. And once you're hooked, it is so very hard to get off these drugs and the spiral down is so quick."[21]

A rally of the Coalition Against Rx Drug Epidemic (CARE) works to call attention to prescription drug misuse.

doctors' prescription pads to write forged prescriptions for themselves. Others purchase drugs from dealers, whose tablets may not contain what they claim.

CHAPTER FOUR

OPIOIDS

Opioids—both legal and illicit—are among the most abused drugs in the United States. They were responsible for 33,000 of the 52,000 drug-related deaths in 2015.[1] Of deaths involving opioid overdose, nearly half involved the use of prescription opioids.

Opiates are drugs derived directly from substances found naturally in the opium poppy, whereas opioids are created synthetically. Morphine, codeine, and thebaine are all opiates. Semisynthetic opioids such as heroin and oxycodone are artificially altered forms of natural opiates. Synthetic opioids are manufactured

Opium poppies are grown and harvested to produce opiates such as morphine and codeine.

substances that do not use any part of the opium poppy. These substances have a chemical structure similar to that of natural opiates and produce similar effects in the body. Meperidine, fentanyl, and methadone are synthetic opioids.

Of the 250 species of poppy in the world, only two produce opium.

PAIN RELIEF

Opioids are powerful pain relievers prescribed for severe pain that does not respond to over-the-counter pain medications. Opioids might be prescribed after surgery or to treat cancer pain, for example. In recent years, opioids have also been prescribed to treat chronic pain.

Although opioids are often prescribed for legitimate health needs, some people feel that this category of drug has been overprescribed since the 1990s. In 1991, 76 million opioid prescriptions were written in the United States.[2] By 2016, that number had increased to 336 million prescriptions.[3] One force driving the increase was the claim by the American Pain Society and the American Academy of Pain Management that doctors were not adequately treating pain. As a result, in the 1990s, pain was named a fifth vital sign, along with blood pressure, pulse, respiratory rate, and oxygen level. Doctors quickly increased opioid prescription rates. "If patients were not totally rid of their pain, that implied the physician was not doing his or her job or really didn't care," said Dr. Jack Ende, president of the American College of Physicians. "That movement went way beyond proper medical care, so much so that there was a lot of overprescription of opioids for noncancer pain."[4] At the same time, pharmaceutical companies—and many doctors—began to promote the use of opioids for chronic pain, despite limited evidence of their long-term effectiveness.

OPIOIDS IN THE BODY

The human body produces natural opioids, known as endogenous opioids. These chemicals attach to opioid receptors on neurons to provide a level of natural pain relief and produce feelings of well-being. Opioid drugs also attach to the

PAIN MEDICATIONS AND FOOTBALL

Football players' bodies take a beating, and many turn to opioid pain relievers prescribed by team doctors to deal with the pain. Often, players take the medications so they can return to the field before their injury is healed, causing greater damage in the long run. Some players report playing through pain out of fear they would be cut from the team. According to former National Football League (NFL) player Austin King, "There is a pervasive culture in football that you must do whatever it takes to get on the field. . . . If you don't show the coaches you will play with pain . . . they will replace you with somebody who will. . . . If you know they'll get rid of you unless you practice, you ask for painkillers."[5]

In 2015, more than 1,800 former NFL players filed a lawsuit against the NFL, claiming that players were pressured to take pain medications and were not adequately informed of the risk of addiction.[6] As of 2017, much of the lawsuit was dismissed.

brain's opioid receptors, but their effects can be much stronger than those of endogenous opioids.

Many people abuse opioids for their tendency to produce feelings of euphoria and relaxation as they activate the brain's opioid receptors. But activation of the opioid receptors also slows normal body functions including breathing and heart rate— sometimes to the point of death. Other side effects of opioids include drowsiness, confusion, dizziness, nausea, vomiting, and constipation. Researchers are also studying the long-term effects of opioid abuse. Some believe that because opioids slow breathing, they restrict the amount of oxygen to the brain. This may lead to permanent brain damage. In addition, some patients who use opioids for chronic pain actually experience an increased sensitivity to pain over time. This effect is known as hyperalgesia. Among the most serious long-term effects of opioids is addiction. After using opioids for only a short time, an individual may find it hard to stop taking the drugs.

PAINKILLERS CAN LEAD TO HEROIN

Daniel Potter, an Indianapolis, Indiana, resident who was formerly addicted, explained the part painkillers played on the road to his heroin addiction. "The bad part about it is everyone I know that is or was addicted to heroin, started with pain pills that were prescribed by a doctor. I haven't heard one person say, 'Yeah, I just decided one day that it would be a good day to start doing heroin.' . . . I can guarantee not a single heroin addict said, 'When I grow up I want to be a junkie.' I never wanted addiction or any of the hell I brought on myself because of it."[7]

COMMONLY ABUSED OPIOIDS

The most commonly abused prescription opioids include hydrocodone, oxycodone, morphine, and codeine. Many opioids come in the form of a tablet, but opioid abusers often crush the tablets to snort the powder or mix it with a liquid to inject it, producing faster, more intense reactions. Some opioid medications come in the form of a liquid, skin patch, or even a lollipop. Street names for prescription opioids include happy pills, hillbilly heroin, oxy, percs, and vikes.

Hydrocodone is the most frequently prescribed—and abused—prescription opioid. In 2017, approximately 58.4 million

Hydrocodone has become one of the first drugs teenagers will experiment with because the tablets are easier to obtain than many other opioids.

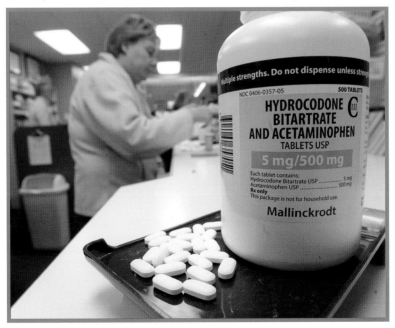

prescriptions were issued for hydrocodone in the United States.[8] This semisynthetic drug is developed from codeine but is six times stronger. It is sold under the brand names Vicodin, Lorcet, Norco, and Lortab. Formerly a Schedule III drug, hydrocodone was rescheduled to Schedule II in 2014. According to former DEA administrator Michele Leonhart, "These products are some of the most addictive and potentially dangerous prescription medications available."[9]

Oxycodone is the next most frequently abused semisynthetic opioid after hydrocodone. It is sold under the names OxyContin, Percocet, and Percodan. OxyContin is an extended-release version of oxycodone, meaning the medication is slowly and evenly distributed to the body over a period of 12 hours. Although this means fewer side effects for those taking the tablets as prescribed, it also means each tablet contains much more oxycodone than shorter-acting formulas. A short-acting tablet may contain only 5 milligrams of oxycodone, for example, while an extended-release OxyContin may have up to 160 milligrams of the drug. Extended-release tablets appeal to abusers who crush and then snort or inject the drugs, taking in a single hit a dose intended to last 12 hours. This drastically increases the risk for addiction and overdose.

Morphine was the first drug ever extracted from opium, and it continues to be one of the most effective and widely prescribed drugs for treating severe pain. It also continues to be

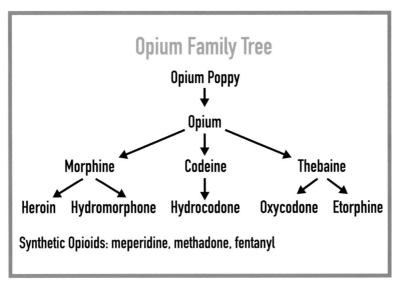

The opium poppy is used to make opium derivatives such as morphine and codeine. Synthetic opioids contain no opium but have a chemical structure similar to that of opium.

widely abused, often through injection. Although less potent than morphine, codeine is often abused as well, usually by taking large quantities of cough medications containing the opioid.

TRANSITIONING TO ILLEGAL OPIOIDS

Recent studies have indicated a link between prescription opioid abuse and use of the illicit opioid heroin. Heroin is a semisynthetic opioid produced from morphine. It acts on the brain and body in the same way as prescription opioids.

Nearly 80 percent of heroin users report using prescription drugs before turning to heroin.[10] Those who transitioned from prescription drugs to heroin said that heroin was often cheaper and easier to obtain than prescription medications. As one woman who turned from prescription drugs to heroin said, "I went back to the doctor a couple times . . . then I started buying OxyContin off the street. . . . OxyContin started to be more expensive and harder to find. A girlfriend of mine introduced me to heroin. I could get a whole lot more for a whole lot less."[11]

The even more powerful synthetic opioid fentanyl has also seen rapidly growing abuse. A prescription drug used to treat cancer pain, fentanyl is 100 times more potent than morphine and 40 times stronger than heroin. Because prescription fentanyl is tightly regulated, most of the fentanyl being abused is an illicit form of the drug produced in secret and illegal labs. Fentanyl is often mixed into heroin or cocaine or sold as a counterfeit prescription opioid. In 2016, the United States experienced a surge in fentanyl-related deaths, with an estimated 20,000 people dying of fentanyl overdose.[12] In 2017, federal officials declared fentanyl "an even more dangerous threat" than heroin.[13] Just 0.25 milligrams—a dose the size of a grain of salt—can be fatal.

DANGERS TO FIRST RESPONDERS

In 2017, the DEA issued a warning to first responders who might come into contact with fentanyl. In its powder form, fentanyl often looks the same as heroin. But accidentally inhaling or ingesting even a small amount of the drug could lead to serious harm. Police were also warned to be careful not to allow drug-sniffing dogs to inhale fentanyl. Many police units began carrying naloxone in case of an accidental overdose by an officer or a dog.

OPIOID OVERDOSE AND NALOXONE

Because of their potency, both prescription and illicit opioids often cause overdose, leading to death. Signs of an overdose can appear 20 minutes to two hours after an individual has used a drug. Symptoms include slowed or stopped breathing, slowed or stopped heartbeat, inability to wake up, and low blood pressure. Additional symptoms include slurred speech, pinpoint pupils, limp body, and blue fingernails or lips. An opioid overdose is a medical emergency.

Emergency medical personnel in many cities have begun to carry naloxone. So have family members and close friends of those at risk of an overdose. Naloxone is an opioid antagonist. This means it can bind to opioid receptors and block the effects of other opioids. Naloxone can reverse the effects of an opioid overdose and restore breathing.

RETHINKING PROMOTION OF PAIN MEDICATIONS

Dr. Russell Portenoy led the movement for increased use of opioid pain medications in the 1990s. He frequently cited a study indicating there was less than a 1 percent risk of addiction to these drugs. In 2010, Portenoy said he shouldn't have used this figure, as it was based on a small sample of patients using opioids short-term in a hospital setting. "I gave innumerable lectures in the late 1980s and '90s about addiction that weren't true," Portenoy said. "Clearly, if I had an inkling of what I know now then, I wouldn't have spoken in the way that I spoke. It was clearly the wrong thing to do."[14]

CHAPTER FIVE

STIMULANTS

Stimulants are substances that increase the activity of the central nervous system. They include legal substances such as caffeine, as well as illicit drugs such as cocaine and methamphetamine. The most commonly abused prescription stimulants are amphetamines and methylphenidate, both Schedule II synthetic drugs. Brand names for these drugs include Adderall (amphetamine) and Ritalin (methylphenidate). On the street, they may be known as bennies, black beauties, skippy, smart drugs, vitamin R, roses, hearts, or uppers.

ADHD TREATMENT

Amphetamines were first synthesized in 1887, and by the 1930s, they were being used to treat asthma, low blood

Adderall is an amphetamine that is commonly prescribed to treat ADHD.

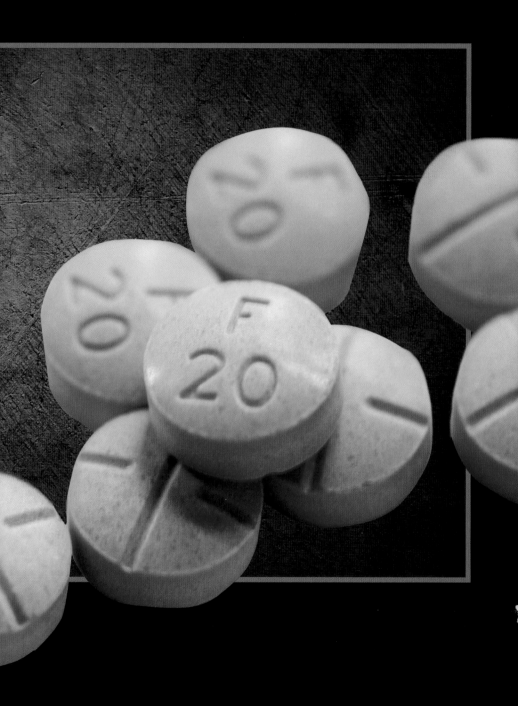

STIMULANTS AND E-SPORTS

The misuse of drugs to improve athletic performance has long been acknowledged as a problem. But in recent years, the problem has spread from the field to the game console. Professional E-Sports players, who compete in fast-paced, intense video games, have to be in top mental form to win the huge prizes up for grabs. To gain a competitive advantage, some players have turned to prescription stimulants such as Adderall. According to professional player Tyler Mozingo, taking Adderall makes "you feel untouchable in a game."[1]

After a top E-Sports player admitted to using Adderall in a tournament in 2015, the Electronic Sports League announced it would begin drug testing its players. The organization said that the drugs gave players an unfair advantage, much like the use of steroids in sports. The drug test involves collecting samples of players' saliva and can detect pain relievers, heroin, marijuana, cocaine, and amphetamines. Other gaming organizations such as Major League Gaming have banned the use of performance-enhancing drugs but do not test for their use.

pressure, and narcolepsy. In 1937, doctors began using these drugs to treat what is now known as ADHD. Although the use of amphetamines for most conditions has declined, amphetamine prescriptions to treat ADHD grew in popularity beginning in the late 1990s.

ADHD is characterized by an inability to concentrate, distractibility, and forgetfulness. Researchers believe that ADHD is caused by an imbalance of specific neurotransmitters in the brain. Amphetamines are believed to correct this imbalance, improving focus and concentration and reducing hyperactivity in those diagnosed with ADHD.

AMPHETAMINE ABUSE

Amphetamines have been abused almost since the time

A growing number of college students are misusing stimulants such as Adderall in order to stay awake and alert longer to study.

they were synthesized. People quickly realized their potential to increase energy and reduce fatigue and the need for sleep. Amphetamines were especially popular during World War II. Soldiers on both sides took them to increase endurance. After the war, factory workers, housewives, truckers, and athletes all found ways to misuse the drugs to stay awake, improve performance, or lose weight. By 1965, federal laws removed many of these products from the market and enacted tighter controls on others.

Today, amphetamines and other stimulants such as methylphenidate are abused largely by college and high school students who take the drugs to help them concentrate and stay awake to study. These drugs are especially prevalent at the end of semesters, when students need to cram for finals. An increasing number of adults also abuse stimulants to deal with high-pressure jobs and long work hours.

Although many people misuse stimulants to improve their school or job performance, recent studies indicate that amphetamines do not improve the ability to learn in individuals not diagnosed with ADHD. Some argue that the feeling of improved performance is a result of impaired judgment rather than an actual improvement in cognitive ability. In fact, college students who abuse ADHD drugs tend to have lower grades than those who do not misuse prescription stimulants.

Some college students also abuse stimulants to help them stay out partying later. Others use the drug to get high or increase feelings of self-esteem. Most stimulants come in tablet form, although some users crush and snort or inject them. Some mix powdered amphetamine with tobacco or marijuana and smoke it.

CHEATING WITH AMPHETAMINES

Besides risking jail sentences or fines, those who misuse prescription stimulants may also find themselves kicked out of school. In the face of widespread amphetamine abuse on college campuses, many schools, including Duke University, have redefined cheating to include the unauthorized use of prescription medication to enhance performance. Some students feel that such policies are unfair. They say taking a stimulant is not the same as cheating on a test but is more like getting extra help from a friend on homework assignments.

AMPHETAMINE IN THE BODY

Similar to the illegal drug cocaine, prescription amphetamines cause the body to release the neurotransmitters dopamine and norepinephrine. These speed up the body's activities, increasing feelings of alertness, focus, and energy. Increased dopamine levels can also lead to feelings of pleasure. Physically, stimulants increase heart rate, respiration, and blood pressure. They can also cause headache, nausea, dizziness, nervousness, inability to sleep, irritability, and weight loss. More serious side effects include depression, dangerously high body temperature, or irregular heartbeat. Long-term amphetamine or methylphenidate users can suffer a type of psychosis that results in paranoia, picking at the skin, and hallucinations. High doses of amphetamines may cause brain damage.

Frequent users can build up a tolerance to amphetamines and need to take higher dosages over time to get the same effects. As the amphetamine wears off, the body's stores of neurotransmitters are depleted, leaving the user feeling fatigued and lethargic. The exhaustion that follows use of a stimulant may lead the user to take another dose, not to get high but simply to have enough energy to get out of bed. Long-term users of amphetamines report experiencing anhedonia, or the inability to feel pleasure without the drug in their system. This feeling can last for months after the user stops taking the drug.

Amphetamine overdose can lead to seizures, heart failure, and death, especially if combined with other drugs. People as young as 15 have died of heart attacks induced by an Adderall or stimulant overdose. Signs of amphetamine overdose include fever, rapid or irregular heartbeat, shallow breathing, enlarged pupils, sweating, and tremors. Amphetamine overdose is a medical emergency that requires immediate care in an emergency room.

MISUSE OF DRUGS IN THE MILITARY

The US military continues to rely on amphetamines. In 2010, active-duty soldiers received 30,000 prescriptions for Adderall, Ritalin, and other stimulants.[2] US Air Force pilots are given "go pills," or amphetamines, to stay awake and alert during long flights. Many soldiers also consume large quantities of energy drinks, which contain the stimulant caffeine. The use of such stimulants is intended to improve soldiers' performance, but some worry that military personnel have not been adequately warned about the dangers of these substances.

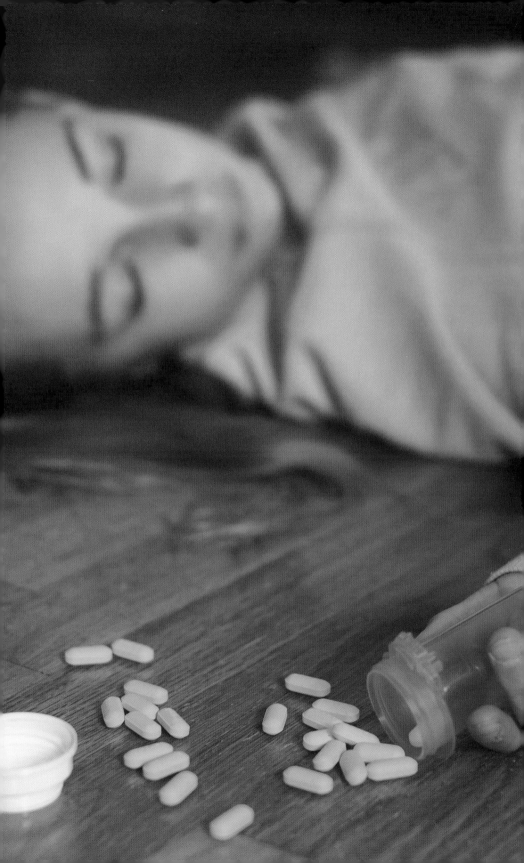

DEPRESSANTS

Central nervous system depressants slow the action of the central nervous system. Alcohol is an example of a depressant substance. Prescription depressants include barbiturates, benzodiazepines, and nonbenzodiazepine sleep medications. These drugs are most often prescribed to treat sleep disorders or anxiety.

After opioids, depressants are among the most abused prescription drugs. In 2015, 7.1 million adults reported misusing prescription depressants at least once during the previous year.[1] Most said they had used the drugs to help them relax or fall asleep. Others abused the drugs to counteract the effects of stimulants. Most depressants come in tablet form. Street names

 FINAL ★★★★

DAILY NEWS

NEW YORK'S PICTURE NEWSPAPER ®

5¢

Vol. 44. No. 36   Copr. 1962 News Syndicate Co. Inc.   New York 17, N.Y., Monday, August 6, 1962★   WEATHER: Fair.

MARILYN DEAD

Marilyn Monroe: "I was never used to being happy."   (NEWS foto by John Duprey)

THE MONROE SAGA: 7 PAGES OF STORIES AND PICTURES

TRUTH SERUM?

In the movies, truth serum can have criminals spilling the truth about their bad deeds. This is actually the barbiturate thiopental, also sometimes called sodium pentothal. It was once used as an anesthetic. Because of its hypnotic qualities, the drug has also been used in attempts to get people to tell the truth. The drug cannot prevent people from lying. Instead, because it slows the speed at which the body's neurons send messages, it makes it harder for a person to concentrate on coming up with a plausible lie. The drug also lowers users' inhibitions, making them more likely to say something they wouldn't admit while not under the drug's influence. It also gives subjects a friendly feeling toward their interrogator.

In 2007, two men in India suspected of multiple murders confessed to the killings after receiving the drug. In the United States, confessions obtained through the use of truth serum were banned in 1963. But in 2012, a judge allowed a Colorado man convicted of killing 12 people to be administered sodium pentothal to determine whether his claim of insanity was true.

for these drugs include A-minus, barbs, candy, downers, phennies, red birds, yellow jackets, or zombie pills.

DEPRESSANTS IN THE BODY

Depressants work by increasing release of the neurotransmitter gamma aminobutyric acid (GABA). This neurotransmitter slows the transmission of nerve messages from one neuron to another. This in turn slows bodily activity and creates a drowsy or calm feeling. Side effects of depressants include slurred speech, shallow breathing, sleepiness, disorientation, headache, light-headedness, and loss of coordination. Depressants slow the heart rate and respiration, and overdose can lead to death, especially when combined with alcohol or other drugs.

Depressants can also cause physical dependence and addiction. Users build up a tolerance to the drugs, needing to take more to feel the same effects. Breaking free of physical dependence is difficult and requires a doctor's supervision, as abruptly stopping the use of some depressants can lead to seizures and even death.

BARBITURATES

Barbiturates were first synthesized in 1864 from barbituric acid. Today, they are sold under brand names such as Mebaral, Nembutal, and Amytal. These drugs are used to treat anxiety and sleep disorders. They are also used for epileptic seizures and as an anesthetic before some surgeries.

Barbiturates are categorized into three groups based on how long their effects last. Long-acting barbiturates last 12 to 24 hours and are used for mild anxiety or seizures. Intermediate or short-acting barbiturates last six to seven hours. They are often used for short-term treatment of sleep disorders or as a sedative before surgery. Ultrashort-acting barbiturates cause unconsciousness within a minute of injection and are used in anesthesia. Those who abuse barbiturates tend to prefer intermediate or short-acting drugs.

In lower doses, the effects of barbiturates are similar to those of alcohol. They can cause euphoria, sleepiness, and a lack of inhibitions, making a person seem drunk. Higher doses can lead to memory problems, lack of coordination, irritability, paranoia, and suicidal thoughts. Long-term use can lead to anxiety, nervousness, a staggering walk, trembling hands, and feelings of hostility leading to violence.

A fatal overdose of barbiturates can occur easily. Users quickly develop a tolerance to these drugs, leading them to take larger and larger amounts. In addition, the dose needed to feel an effect is extremely close to a lethal dose. Signs of a barbiturate overdose include cold but sweaty skin, a weak pulse, slow breathing, and loss of reflexes. A barbiturate overdose is a medical emergency and requires immediate medical intervention. Barbiturate overdose can quickly lead to coma, permanent brain damage, respiratory failure,

WITHDRAWAL

Substance misuse can happen quickly. Oftentimes, people don't realize they are misusing until they have formed an addiction. Patricia, a former Xanax abuser, explained, "I realized I was using more Xanax on a regular basis. I took time off work to get off it. Without the knowledge I was addicted, I went 'cold turkey.' For four days and nights I was bedridden. I didn't sleep or eat. I vomited. I had hallucinations. On about the third day without Xanax, I started to become uncoordinated and unbalanced and bumped into things. On about the fourth day I became really worried when I started having twitching sensations."[2]

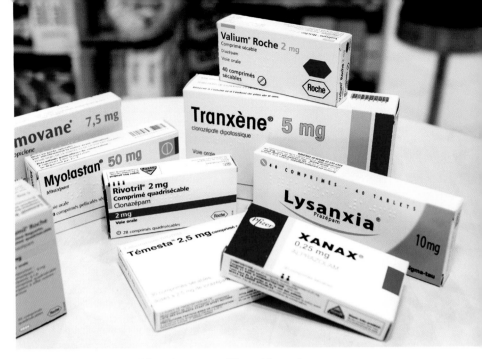

Benzodiazepines are sold under many different brand names.

and death. Sudden withdrawal from barbiturates can also lead to death.

BENZODIAZEPINES

Because of barbiturates' high risk of overdose, both their legitimate and illegal use has fallen in popularity. In many cases, they have been replaced by depressants known as benzodiazepines. First synthesized in the 1950s, these drugs were believed to be less addictive than barbiturates. In addition, there is a wider margin between the therapeutic dose—the dose needed to produce effects—and the fatal dose. This fact makes these drugs safer for those who take them as prescribed.

Benzodiazepines are sold under brand names such as Valium, Xanax, Halcion, Ativan, and Klonopin. They are used to treat anxiety, panic attacks, and sleep disorders. In some cases, they can also be prescribed for restless legs syndrome, epileptic seizures, and cerebral palsy. Because of their potential for addiction, these drugs are not usually prescribed for long-term treatment.

Side effects of benzodiazepines are similar to those of barbiturates and include drowsiness, confusion, dizziness, light-headedness, and slurred speech. They can also cause memory problems, irritability, and depression. Unlike barbiturates, benzodiazepines do not have a strong depressant effect on respiration and heart rate. This means they are not often fatal when taken alone. However, when taken in combination with other drugs including alcohol, other depressants, or opioids, fatal respiratory depression can occur. In fact, in 2015, nearly 9,000 people died of benzodiazepine overdose. Almost 80 percent of those deaths involved simultaneous use of benzodiazepines and opioids.[3]

THE DANGER OF SHARING

The guilt of providing a prescription drug to another person who uses it and overdoses can be overwhelming. "I have overdosed twice off of prescription pills (the antipsychotic Zyprexa) and had a close friend die of the same drug," said Zyprexa user Linda. "There is no worse feeling than knowing that your friend is dead because you gave him pills you knew relatively little about."[5]

All the possible side effects of nonbenzodiazepine sleep aids are not yet fully understood.

NONBENZODIAZEPINE SLEEP MEDICATIONS

In recent years, pharmaceutical companies have developed a new class of nonbenzodiazepine sleep medications. Sometimes referred to as z-drugs, these medications are sold under the brand names Ambien, Sonata, and Lunesta and are used to treat sleep disorders. According to some studies, they have fewer side effects and a lower risk of addiction than benzodiazepines. However, other studies and incidents have raised questions about their psychoactive properties.

Side effects of z-drugs include confusion, dizziness, daytime sleepiness, memory problems, and hallucinations. Some people have reported incidents of sleepwalking, sleep eating, and even sleep driving while using some of these drugs.

OVER-THE-COUNTER DRUGS

Over-the-counter (OTC) medications are legal drugs available without a prescription. They can be purchased at pharmacies, grocery stores, and even gas stations. Over-the-counter drugs are often abused by young people because they are relatively cheap and easy to get. Approximately 10 percent of teens in grades 7 to 12 report abusing over-the-counter medications.[1]

Because they are available over the counter, these drugs may also seem safer than prescription drugs. But when used incorrectly, even OTC drugs can cause serious side effects and even death.

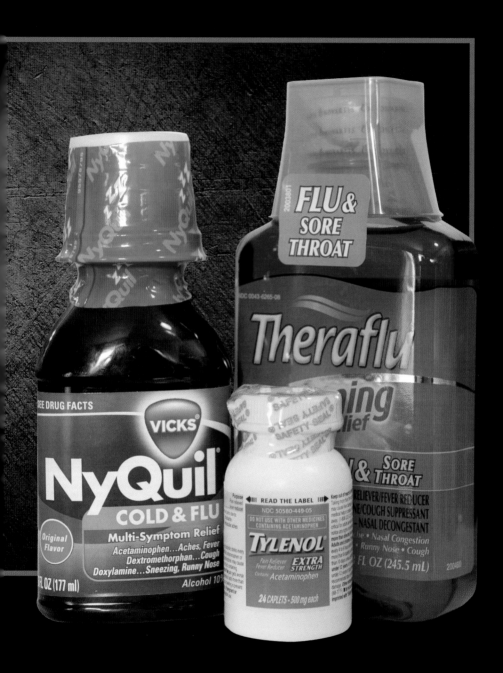

DXM

The most commonly abused OTC medications are cough medicines containing dextromethorphan (DXM). Although not an opioid itself, DXM is a synthetic substance derived from the opioid levomethorphan. It is chemically related to codeine. When taken as directed, it works to prevent coughing by blocking the brain's cough reflex. DXM is an active ingredient in more than 140 OTC medications. Some of these include Alka Seltzer Plus, Coricidin, Mucinex DM, Robitussin, Sudafed, and Tylenol Cough, Cold, and Flu. These medications come in capsule, liquid, lozenge, and tablet form. Powdered DXM is also sometimes sold for research purposes. Street names for the drug include candy, dex, robo, skittles, triple c, drank, vitamin D, and velvet. Those who abuse the drug usually ingest it, but some snort the powdered form. Some people refer to abusing DXM as robotripping.

The effects of DXM depend on the user's size and the amount of the drug taken. Recommended doses for cough

GETTING HOOKED

Addiction can cost users more than money and relationships. Crystal, a DXM abuser, regrets the time she spent being obsessed with getting her next high. "My experience with DXM: I started peeing blood. I felt sick. . . . My body felt weak. . . . I gave up everything because I was obsessed with using. . . . All I cared about was getting high. . . . I thought I could just use Coricidin for fun, that it didn't matter. I never expected to get hooked. . . . I'll never be able to get that time back. If I could erase it and make it go away, I would."[2]

suppression range from 10 to
20 milligrams every four hours.
But those who abuse the drug
may take up to 1,500 milligrams
in a single dose. At low doses,
DXM can create an alcohol-like
intoxication, causing slurred

Some DXM abusers roboshake, or force themselves to drink large quantities of cough syrup and then vomit, because they want to absorb the DXM through the stomach lining without being affected by the other ingredients in the medication.

speech and short-term memory problems. At higher doses, DXM
can cause vivid hallucinations and produce the feeling of floating
outside one's body. DXM also induces feelings of euphoria
and escape.

Side effects of DXM-containing medications include
vomiting, dizziness, and drowsiness. Higher doses of DXM can
cause increased heart rate, blurred vision, and sweating. In some
cases, DXM abuse can cause respiratory depression and death.

Although once considered nonaddictive, new evidence
indicates that DXM may cause addiction. In addition, long-term
use can cause nerve cell damage, bone marrow problems, high
blood pressure, heart damage, and even brain damage.

OTC STIMULANTS

Although some stimulant medications require a prescription,
others are sold over the counter. Many cold medications
contain pseudoephedrine, a stimulant chemically similar to
amphetamine. Used as directed, pseudoephedrine helps clear

nasal congestion. But in higher doses, the drug produces feelings of euphoria or hallucinations. Some people abuse the drug to lose weight or increase their energy level. Side effects of pseudoephedrine abuse include weakness, vomiting, irregular heartbeat, breathing problems, high blood pressure, dizziness, seizures, and heart attacks.

Another type of OTC stimulant is diet pills, which contain stimulants that suppress the appetite. In recent years, the FDA has tightened regulations surrounding OTC diet pills, prohibiting the inclusion of stimulants considered dangerous, such as phenylpropanolamine, ephedrine, and ephedra. However, some diet pills still contain powerful stimulants that produce effects similar to those of the banned substances. Bitter orange, for example, can cause nervousness, rapid heartbeat, and high blood pressure. Stroke, heart failure, and death are also possible. Other side effects of diet pills can include hair loss,

HERBAL SUBSTANCES

Herbal substances can have as strong an effect on the body as prescription and OTC drugs. But they are subject to less scrutiny. Because they are considered dietary supplements, herbal substances do not have to be approved by the FDA. However, the FDA can remove dietary supplements shown to have significant risks from the market. In 2004, for example, the FDA removed diet products containing the herbal supplement ephedra from the market after they caused thousands of deaths. Even so, ephedrine continues to be sold over the internet and abused by people around the world for its stimulant properties.

insomnia, vomiting, and blurred vision. Diet drug abuse often begins with only a few pills, but users increase the dosage over time, leading to addiction.

Caffeine pills are a widely used—and abused—form of OTC stimulant. The caffeine in these pills is the same as that found in coffee, energy drinks, and soda. Caffeine has been shown to cause physical dependence, with those who stop using it experiencing withdrawal symptoms. Although safe when consumed in moderation, ingesting large quantities of caffeine tablets—especially alongside energy drinks—can lead to dehydration, panic attacks, vomiting, and dizziness. More serious effects include irregular heartbeat, hallucinations, convulsions, and breathing problems. In some cases, caffeine overdose has led to death, especially in people with underlying heart problems.

Energy drinks are a popular way to consume high levels of caffeine.

OTHER OTC DRUGS OF ABUSE

Some people have found ways to abuse other types of OTC drugs as well. Some take large quantities of motion sickness pills such as Dramamine or antihistamines such as Benadryl to experience mild euphoria and relaxation. At higher doses, these drugs cause hallucinations. Side effects include drowsiness, headache, blurred vision, ringing ears, nausea, itching, and dizziness. More serious effects include liver and kidney damage, memory loss, and depression. High doses can lead to irregular heartbeat, coma, heart attack, and death.

Some people also abuse antidiarrheal medications such as Imodium or Kaopectate. These medications contain loperamide, an opioid medication that does not enter the brain but instead regulates the intestinal tract. Some opioid abusers reportedly use these OTC medications to deal with opioid withdrawal. In high quantities, these drugs may produce euphoria and other psychoactive effects. High doses can lead to serious health problems, including fainting, abdominal pain, kidney failure, and cardiac arrest.

Some people abuse OTC medications not to get high but out of a desire to increase their effectiveness. Some people take more than the recommended dosage of acetaminophen or ibuprofen, for example, in hopes of greater pain relief. But large doses of acetaminophen can cause liver failure, while high doses of ibuprofen can lead to stomach bleeding, kidney failure, and cardiac problems.

People who have difficulty sleeping may turn to OTC sleeping pills. Although these pills are meant to be taken for only a few nights in a row, many people continue to take them for much longer. Side effects of OTC sleeping medications include drowsiness, constipation, dizziness, inability to concentrate, and forgetfulness. If a person drives or operates heavy machinery, such side effects can lead to fatal accidents. Long-term use can lead to tolerance, dependence, and even addiction.

MIX IT UP

In addition to being dangerous on their own, OTC drugs are often taken in combination with

OTC LIMITS

Although legal to purchase without a prescription, sales of some OTC drugs have been limited by law or by store policies. Pseudoephedrine, for example, is found in OTC cold medications but is also a key ingredient in the manufacture of methamphetamine. Federal law now requires pharmacies to keep pseudoephedrine products behind the counter. Anyone purchasing these products must show identification and sign for them, though they don't need a prescription. The amount a single buyer can purchase is limited to 3.6 grams a day.

Although not required to by federal law, some stores have also set restrictions on sales of OTC medications containing DXM. Some states prohibit sales of DXM products to anyone under the age of 18. In many places, stores have moved DXM products behind the sales counter to reduce the risk of shoplifting. Some stores also limit the number of DXM-containing products a single customer can purchase.

prescription drugs and alcohol, which increases the likelihood of a fatal overdose. For example, DXM may be taken in combination with the illicit drug ecstasy. Together, the two drugs may increase body temperature to life-threatening levels.

In other cases, young people mix DXM cough medicines with alcohol and sometimes crushed prescription painkillers, creating a potentially fatal mixture. Others mix cough medicines containing the opioid codeine with alcohol or soft drinks and candy. The resulting concoction—known as sizzurp, lean, syrup, or purple drank—can slow breathing and heart rate and lead to death.

DXM is the active ingredient in approximately 140 commercially available cough medications and is widely available. Although DXM was developed over 50 years ago, abuse has increased dramatically in the last five years. The National Capital Poison Center reports that abuse of DXM leads to approximately 6,000 emergency room visits per year. Around 50 percent of these visits are from people ages 12–25.[3] It is likely that many more cases of

DXM APP

The Partnership for Drug-Free Kids and the Consumer Healthcare Products Association have teamed up to create an app that allows users to experience the effects of DXM without trying the drug themselves. Called DXM Labworks, the app allows users to guide a robot high on DXM through a series of challenges. The robot simulates effects of DXM abuse, including vomiting, disorientation, and dizziness.

Purchases of OTC pseudoephedrine are now monitored closely because it is used in the manufacturing of methamphetamines.

misusing DXM are never reported if the abuser does not develop symptoms severe enough to require emergency medical care.

At "pharming" parties—also known as skittles parties—young people may dump a mix of prescription and OTC drugs into a bag and then take a handful. They don't know what drugs they are taking. The use of these drugs may be combined with robotripping or drinking alcohol, increasing the danger of a fatal overdose.

CHAPTER EIGHT

ADDICTION AND TREATMENT

Abuse of prescription drugs can lead to substance use disorder, or addiction. According to the Substance Abuse and Mental Health Services Administration (SAMHSA), "Substance use disorders occur when the recurrent use of alcohol and/or drugs causes clinically and functionally significant impairment, such as health problems, disability, and failure to meet major responsibilities at work, school, or home."[1]

In 2016, an estimated 2.1 million people in the United States had an opioid use disorder. Of that number, about 1.8 million had a prescription opioid use disorder, with the remainder facing a heroin use disorder.[2] An additional 618,000 people had a

Opiate addiction is one of the biggest health issues facing Americans today.

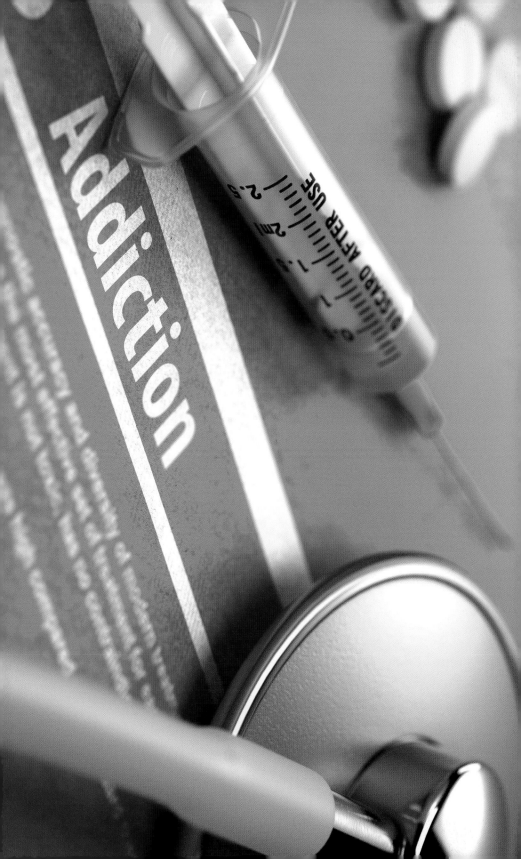

tranquilizer use disorder, with 540,000 dealing with stimulant use disorder.[3]

TOLERANCE AND DEPENDENCE

Two of the characteristics of substance use disorder are tolerance and dependence on a drug. Tolerance is the need to take more of a drug over time to get the same effects. Physical dependence occurs when the body gets so used to the presence of a drug that users experience physical symptoms, known as withdrawal, if they stop taking it. Opioid withdrawal is characterized by flu-like symptoms, including watery eyes, runny nose, muscle and bone pain, diarrhea, vomiting, cold flashes, and sleep problems. Additional symptoms may include loss of appetite, increased heart rate and blood pressure, restlessness, and uncontrollable leg movements. Depressant withdrawal symptoms can include anxiety, headaches, dizziness, loss of appetite, sleep problems, weakness, and tremors.

SIGNS OF A PROBLEM

Experts have identified a number of signs that may indicate a drug abuse problem. These include changes in behavior, lower performance at work or in school, and changing friends. Drug abuse issues can also cause a lack of concern about appearance, losing interest in hobbies and activities, and changing eating or sleeping habits. Family and friends might also notice a person at risk of addiction acting secretive or suspicious, and experiencing periods of giddiness or paranoia. Physical signs may include sudden weight loss or gain, slurred speech, or bloodshot eyes.

Sudden withdrawal from depressants can be life threatening, causing hallucinations, seizures, shock, and death. Stimulant withdrawal can cause tiredness, lack of energy, muscle and abdominal pains, chills, hunger, irritability, anxiety, depression, and suicidal thoughts.

ADDICTION

In many cases, drug dependence leads to addiction. According to the American Society of Addiction Medicine, addiction is a "chronic disease of brain reward, motivation, memory, and related circuitry."[4]

In the past, many people considered drug addiction to be a sign of moral weakness on the part of the user. But in recent years, scientists have discovered addiction is a disease that affects both the brain and behavior. Brain imaging studies have shown changes in the brains of people with the disease of addiction, specifically in areas that control memory, learning, decision-making, and judgment. Although a person makes a choice to use a drug the first time, once the brain has been rewired, the choice to continue using the drug may be taken out of the person's hands as the brain's self-control system is impaired. According to J. W. Wilson, executive director of the Advanced Learning Institute, "Your brain

Among the earliest known people addicted to morphine were Alexander Wood—inventor of the hypodermic needle—and his wife.

structures for your drug of choice become very similar in biology to your need for air, food, and water. . . . The feeling to the addict is the same as if I tried to strangle you and wouldn't give you oxygen. You would do anything you could to get that oxygen. That's why addicts do things that in an unaddicted state they would never do."[5]

Drugs become the most important thing in an addicted person's life. They may recognize the harmful effects of their drug abuse on their health, family, and life, but they continue to misuse drugs anyway. According to pain management doctor Deeni Bassam, continuing to take a drug even while realizing its harmful consequences is a key sign of addiction: "How do you know you're an addict? It's when you're doing something that you know is not good for you, that's harming you, but you can't help yourself. . . . When your relationships are starting to fall apart around you, and you don't

THE TRUTH ABOUT ADDICTION

Erin Marie Daly lost her younger brother Pat after his OxyContin addiction ended in a heroin overdose. After his death, Daly interviewed people with addictions and wrote a book entitled *Generation Rx: A Story of Dope, Death, and America's Opiate Crisis.* She wrote, "Not one addict I interviewed mentioned the word fun in connection with his or her addiction. By contrast, they knew they were hurting everyone around them, and they hated themselves for it. They lived a tortured existence that paired this horrible realization with a physical dependence on a drug that would send them into excruciating fits of withdrawal if they failed to get their next dose."[6]

care. And the only thing that's on your mind is about how to get the substance and how to get the next high."[7]

ADDICTION TREATMENT

Because addiction is a brain disease, quitting requires more than a desire to stop using. Most people who are addicted to drugs require formal treatment to stop using and return to a healthy lifestyle. Addiction treatment may occur in an outpatient program, in which an individual continues to live at home but attends treatment appointments. It may also occur in an inpatient program involving a stay in the hospital or a residential treatment facility.

Treatment usually begins with a period of detoxification, or detox. During this time, the user stops taking the drug. Doctors and treatment specialists oversee the detoxification process to make sure the person is able to stop using the drug safely and to help manage withdrawal symptoms. In the case of depressants, the patient's dose of the drug must slowly be decreased over time to prevent potentially fatal seizures. Patients going through opioid withdrawal may be given a less psychoactive opioid such as methadone to help prevent withdrawal symptoms.

Detoxification is only the first step in drug treatment. Another important part of treatment is behavioral therapy. This can include individual, family, or group counseling in which the patient works with a counselor to change his or her behavior and

Group counseling can help those addicted to prescription drugs by teaching healthy coping skills to better manage daily stressors that could lead to repeat substance abuse.

attitudes regarding drug use. The counselor may help the patient learn coping strategies for stressful situations, practice avoiding drug use, determine strategies for dealing with drug cravings, and develop healthy life skills.

MEDICATION-ASSISTED TREATMENT

Some treatment programs for opioid use disorder use medication-assisted treatment (MAT) alongside behavioral therapies. MAT involves the use of medications that can relieve drug cravings or block the effects of opioids. Drugs used in MAT include methadone, buprenorphine, and naltrexone.

Methadone has been used to treat opioid use disorder for nearly 50 years. It is an opioid agonist, meaning it binds to opioid receptors in the brain in the same way as other opioid drugs. But its effects on the release of dopamine are much milder, so it doesn't cause the intense high of other opioid drugs. Methadone helps reduce patients' withdrawal symptoms and drug cravings by tricking the brain into thinking it is still getting the drugs it wants.

The semisynthetic opioid buprenorphine is considered a partial opioid agonist because it attaches to opioid receptors but only partially activates them. Buprenorphine does not produce the strong euphoria or other side effects of other opioids. Like methadone, it is used to reduce withdrawal symptoms and drug cravings.

Naloxone and naltrexone are opioid antagonists. These drugs bind to opioid receptors but

ARGUMENTS OVER MAT

Some critics of MAT argue that this type of treatment simply substitutes one type of drug addiction for another, and only prolongs the problem. "Ten or 20 years from now, they're going to look at this as the Dark Ages of rehab, because people have bought into the line that the only way to deal with this is to keep these people on medication," said Vann Ellison, president of St. Matthew's House recovery program in Florida. "But we've known for decades that getting them off mood-altering chemicals leads to a productive, healthy, and independent life."[8]

The Partnership for Drug-Free Kids takes a different view. According to a statement by the organization, "Taking medication for opioid addiction is like taking medication for any other chronic disease, such as diabetes or asthma. When it is used according to the doctor's instructions, the medication will not create a new addiction."[9] According to some studies, treatments that combine medication and behavioral counseling are more effective than either type of treatment on its own.

do not activate them. They block other opioids from attaching to the receptors. Naloxone acts quickly and for a short period of time and is most often used to treat overdoses. Naltrexone is a longer-term treatment to prevent relapse of opioid use. If a person using naltrexone takes another opioid drug, the naltrexone will prevent them from feeling the sought-after high from the drug.

Some medications use a combination of buprenorphine and naloxone. The buprenorphine reduces withdrawal symptoms and drug cravings, while the naloxone prevents abuse by causing withdrawal symptoms if a user attempts to inject the drug. Recent studies indicate these combination drugs may be among the most successful opioid addiction treatments.

RELAPSE

The goal of substance use disorder treatment is to return

SAFELY TAKING PRESCRIPTION PAINKILLERS

Many people who become addicted to opioids began by taking a legitimately prescribed painkiller. Despite their potential for addiction, prescription opioids are still the most effective painkillers known to medicine. In some cases, they are the only medication that can help with severe pain. Doctors offer several tips to help those prescribed painkillers keep from becoming addicted. These include taking only the prescribed amount, reducing the dosage taken over time, and requesting abuse-deterrent medications. Properly disposing of leftover pills is also important. If you feel as though you can't stop taking the drugs, tell a friend, family member, or doctor.

Recovering prescription drug addicts have a higher rate of relapse when they lack a family support system.

the patient to a productive, safe, drug-free life. But even with treatment, many people continue to struggle with addiction and relapses. In fact, an estimated 40 to 60 percent of those who seek addiction treatment relapse. The rate may be as high as 90 percent among those addicted to opioids.[10]

Cravings for drugs can continue long after a person last used them. This is in part because of the way drugs work in the brain and how the brain responds in their absence. Withdrawal from opioids can cause feelings of dysphoria, the opposite of euphoria. Stimulant withdrawal can produce anhedonia. Both dysphoria and anhedonia can last for weeks or months, leading former users to return to taking the drugs.

CHAPTER NINE

IMPACT ON SOCIETY

The misuse of prescription drugs costs the United States an estimated $78.5 billion per year. This includes an estimated $26 billion in health-care costs.[1] Other costs include lost productivity at work, increased costs related to policing of drug-related crimes, and the cost of foster care for children whose parents are addicted to drugs.

HEALTH-CARE COSTS

Prescription drug misuse adds to health-care costs for individuals, hospitals, and taxpayers. These costs include added expenses for emergency responses to overdose calls.

Michelle Holley holds a picture of her daughter, Jaime Holley, who died in 2016 at the age of 19 from an overdose.

Many cities have also incurred the expense of carrying additional naloxone on all emergency vehicles to reverse opioid overdoses. Hospital-related costs for some patients are covered by Medicaid and other government-funded programs. According to some estimates, up to one-quarter of all Medicaid dollars are spent on drug-related health expenses brought about by misuse of medications.[2]

The increase in drug overdoses is not the only issue straining health-care resources. The use of needles to inject drugs has also resulted in an explosion in cases of human immunodeficiency virus (HIV) and hepatitis C infection in many areas. HIV is a virus that attacks the immune system. Hepatitis C is a liver infection that can lead to liver failure.

In 2014, an outbreak of HIV tore through the small town of Austin, Indiana. Within months, 194 people were infected with the disease. This was nearly 5 percent of the town's population of 4,200.[3] According to health officials, 100 percent of the new cases of HIV were a result of sharing needles to inject prescription opioids. Cases of hepatitis C—a disease even more infectious than HIV—have increased as well. Occurrences of this liver disease tripled in the space of only a few years, mainly because of needle use among young drug abusers. Treatment for a patient infected with HIV or hepatitis C can reach $100,000 to $300,000 or more over the person's lifetime, adding to the financial cost of drug abuse.[4]

IN THE WORKPLACE

Prescription drug abuse also has a significant impact on the country's workforce. According to a 2011 study, lost earnings and employment related to the abuse of prescription drugs costs the country $25.6 billion a year.[5]

An employee's drug use affects both coworkers and business owners. Coworkers may have to work longer hours or take additional responsibilities to make up for the lost work of a drug-abusing employee. Employees who show up to work while high are an estimated one-third less productive than other employees.[6] They can also be a danger to others if they have to operate vehicles or heavy machinery.

Prescription drug misuse can also make it difficult for users to find and retain work. According

BABIES IN WITHDRAWAL

As the opioid epidemic gripped the United States, hospitals across the country reported an increase in the number of babies born with neonatal abstinence syndrome. This is opioid withdrawal that happens when mothers use opioids while pregnant. Signs of neonatal abstinence syndrome include tremors, fevers, seizures, and muscle cramps. Many of these babies are treated in special neonatal units that are kept quiet and dim to avoid overstimulating the babies. When the babies cry, nurses sway slowly side-to-side with them. They avoid smiling at the babies, as even that gesture can be too stimulating. Over the course of several weeks, the babies receive tapered doses of methadone or morphine to help them wean from the drugs until their bodies are no longer dependent on them. Doctors worry about the long-term effects of the drug exposure on these babies, and whether they will suffer consequences later on in life.

to Princeton University economist Alan Krueger, prescription drug abuse has contributed to 20 percent of the overall drop in participation in the labor force, making it a major factor in this demographic shift that also includes the overall aging of the population.[7] These people are unable to work due to drug misuse. Many businesses require employees to undergo routine drug testing before being hired. But in some cities, business owners are finding it difficult to even find enough employees who can pass a drug screening to keep their businesses running.

Lost productivity doesn't only affect employers and employees, according to health-care economist Howard Birnbaum: "If people don't have jobs, they don't have money to spend in the grocery store, on gasoline. . . . The socioeconomic burden is much broader than on any individual or any firm."[8]

FAMILY EFFECTS

The youngest victims of the opioid epidemic are children whose parents misuse opioids or

DRUGGED DRIVING

Misuse of prescription drugs can impair driving in much the same way as alcohol. Prescription depressants and opioids, in particular, can cause drowsiness, dizziness, and slowed reaction time, all of which can impact safety on the road. The number of accidents caused by prescription drug abuse is difficult to determine, however, as there is not a good roadside test for drug use, as there is for alcohol impairment. According to a study published in 2017, the number of drivers killed in car crashes who had prescription medications in their bloodstream at the time of the crash was seven times greater in 2015 than in 1999.[9]

Prescription drug abuse can have a devastating effect on the children of parents with addiction. They may be neglected when the parents' energy is focused on getting high.

other prescription drugs. Many of these children face neglect or abuse as parents deal with drug addiction. "The power that these drugs have over people is unbelievable," according to Aundrea Cordle, director for Job and Family Services in an Ohio county hit hard by the opioid epidemic. "You could have a loving parent who cares deeply for a child. But once that parent gets involved in opioids, it's as if the child no longer exists. Getting the next high is the priority."[10]

Other children are left as orphans when their parents overdose. In 2015, the number of children in foster care nationwide reached 430,000, an 8 percent increase since 2012.[11] An additional 2.7 million children were being raised by grandparents or other relatives.[12] Experts believe much of the increase in the number of children in the care of individuals other than their parents is due to opioid misuse by parents.

DRUGS AND CRIME

Prescription drug abuse also impacts the criminal justice system. More than 50 percent of the federal prison population in the United States is made up of people convicted of drug-related crimes.[13] Criminal justice costs related to the abuse of opioids and other prescription drugs top $7.7 billion a year.[14]

Drug abuse often leads to other crimes as well. People desperate to get their next dose of a prescription drug may resort to stealing it from a doctor's office, pharmacy, or family member's medicine cabinet. Others turn to stealing cell phones, jewelry, or other goods from family members. They sell these goods to get money to purchase drugs. Some employees steal money from their employers.

BLACK MARKET

The desire for prescription drugs also fuels the sale of these drugs—and look-alike products—on the black market.

BIG PROFITS

The easy availability and low cost of fentanyl, combined with the potential for huge profits, spurs the manufacture of counterfeit prescription medications. A kilogram (2.2 lbs) of fentanyl powder costs around $3,000 to obtain from a supplier, usually from China. That kilogram of powder can be pressed into one million counterfeit pills, each containing one milligram of fentanyl. Marked as oxycodone or another prescription medication, the pills can sell for $10 to $20 apiece, resulting in a profit of $10 to $20 million off a single kilogram of fentanyl powder.[15]

Counterfeit, or fake, prescription drugs are often sold illegally by dealers on the street or through internet pharmacies. These drugs may look and be packaged just like those prescribed by a doctor. But they are made in secret labs and usually are not what they claim to be. They may contain dangerous ingredients or the wrong amount of an active ingredient.

Beginning in 2014, an increasing number of counterfeit pills were found to contain the powerful opioid fentanyl. These pills were marked to look like the prescription opioids oxycodone or hydrocodone. Some mimic benzodiazepines such as Xanax. Fentanyl can be deadly even in doses as small as 0.25 milligrams. Counterfeit pills have no standard dosage and can contain as little as 0.6 milligrams or as much as 6.9 milligrams of fentanyl per pill—far beyond a fatal dose.

DRUG ABUSE AND SUICIDE

Among the hidden costs of prescription drug abuse is an increase in suicide rates. After depression and other mood disorders, alcohol and drug abuse are leading risk factors for suicide. Drug use may increase the risk of suicide by amplifying feelings of depression or despair. Along with overdose, suicide is a leading cause of death among substance abusers. In some cases, the substance itself becomes a means for committing suicide. More than 17 percent of all drug overdoses are believed to be intentional, and in 2010, an estimated 202,000 people attempted to use prescription drugs to commit suicide.[16]

Black market drug dealers sometimes mix the synthetic opioid carfentanil, an elephant tranquilizer 100 times more potent than fentanyl, with heroin or other drugs, creating a deadly combination.

CHAPTER TEN

FIGHTING THE CRISIS

The federal government budgets billions of dollars each year to combat drug abuse. In March 2017, President Donald Trump formed the President's Commission on Combating Drug Addiction and the Opioid Crisis. Led by New Jersey governor Chris Christie, the commission issued its first recommendation in August 2017, writing, "Our citizens are dying. We must act boldly to stop it. The first and most urgent recommendation of this Commission is . . . declare a national emergency."[1] In late October 2017, Trump declared the crisis a public health emergency, which is different than a

President Trump signs a presidential memorandum declaring the opioid crisis to be a public health emergency.

WHAT ABOUT PEOPLE WITH PAIN?

According to a 2011 Institute of Medicine study, 100 million Americans suffer from chronic pain.[3] Many of these patients cannot lead normal lives without prescription opioids, which remain the most effective painkillers available. Some experts fear that tighter restrictions on prescription drugs will keep these patients from getting the painkillers they need and lead them to seek opioids—including illicit ones—elsewhere. Others worry the restrictions will sentence them to a life of pain. "If you insist on regulation, then you're consigning my (82-year-old) mother (with arthritis) and millions of others to live in chronic pain," said pain doctor Russell Portenoy.[4] Those who support increased regulation say the intention isn't to eliminate opioids altogether. "It's silly to say opioids are evil. Pain needs to be treated," said Dr. Laurence Westreich, an addiction psychiatrist.[5] Instead, regulations are designed to make doctors more careful about when and how much of these drugs they prescribe.

national emergency. A national emergency would have been a short-term answer to the problem. Declaring it a public health emergency allowed for more funding for long-term solutions. "It is time to liberate our communities from this scourge of drug addiction," the president said. "We can be the generation that ends the opioid epidemic."[2] The emergency declaration allowed for federal grant money to be allocated for the crisis. It also allowed for the expansion of online medical services, which allow people to consult with a doctor online, for residents of rural areas with little access to treatment centers. According to Tom Coderre, a former SAMHSA official, "[The] most beneficial part of having a public health emergency is you really can muster public support and then you can bring all the resources of the federal government to bear on it, bringing people from all of the agencies to combat the issue."[6] Many experts agreed that ending prescription drug abuse would require the combined efforts of governments, scientists, and health-care workers.

PREVENTION AND EDUCATION

One of the first steps to ending prescription drug abuse is to increase prevention efforts, especially among young people. Early substance abuse increases an individual's risk of developing an addiction, so reaching young people with a prevention message is crucial. Yet only 14 percent of teens say their parents have talked to them about the dangers of misusing prescription drugs. In comparison, 81 percent say their parents have warned them about the risks of marijuana.[7] To combat this problem, some schools have developed programs to educate students about the dangers of prescription drugs. In 2014, Ohio passed a law requiring all schools to provide classes on prescription opioid abuse as part of the health curriculum for all grades, beginning in kindergarten.

Prevention efforts do not stop with students, however. Many health-care professionals have only limited training in pain treatment. To remedy that, in 2012, the FDA requested that pharmaceutical companies that produce certain opioid products offer training courses to physicians to review risks and safe prescribing practices. Some states have also passed laws requiring health-care workers to complete training to help them recognize the signs of prescription drug abuse in a patient. Many doctors have also committed to better educating their patients about the dangers of prescription opioids.

DRUG TESTS AT SCHOOL

Some schools have implemented random drug testing programs for students who participate in competitive extracurricular activities such as sports. These tests usually involve providing a urine sample that is then tested for drugs such as marijuana, cocaine, amphetamines, and opioids. Through these tests, schools hope to discourage students from using drugs in the first place, as well as to identify students who may be in need of treatment for a drug problem. Testing positive for drugs may result in suspension from the team or other extracurricular activities.

DRUG MONITORING

Nearly all 50 states have now implemented Prescription Drug Monitoring Programs (PDMPs), databases that track prescriptions of controlled substances. PDMPs record which medications patients are being prescribed, along with who prescribed and dispensed the medications. These databases can flag a patient who has received multiple prescriptions from multiple doctors. They also track doctors who may be overprescribing such medications.

Supporters of PDMPs say they are a key component in reducing drug addiction and overdose. New York state

Drug Deaths by State[9]

Legend:
- 6.9 to 11.0
- 11.1 to 13.5
- 13.6 to 16.0
- 16.1 to 18.5
- 18.6 to 21.0
- 21.1 to 52.0

For every 100,000 people in the United States, 19.8 died of a drug overdose in 2016.

reported a 75 percent decrease in cases of doctor-shopping after requiring doctors to check the state PDMP before issuing prescription painkillers.[8] However, some argue that PDMPs may lead doctors to stop prescribing certain medications for patients who need them because these doctors fear the penalties they could receive.

GREATER ACCESS TO TREATMENT

As prescription opioids become less available, some people turn to illicit opioids such as heroin and fentanyl, leading to an increase in opioid-related deaths. In response, many states and communities have increased their access to the overdose-reversal drug naloxone. Some schools have also begun to keep the drug on hand.

In many cases, a person taken to the emergency room for an overdose is treated and stabilized, then returns home. But efforts are underway to increase the number of people being referred to treatment centers for substance use disorder. Increasing the number of people receiving treatment may require the opening of additional treatment centers, especially in rural areas. In many of these places, local police or emergency departments oversee detoxification of patients. But they do not have the resources to provide ongoing treatment. Patients may have to drive long distances to a treatment facility, making them less likely to seek treatment.

According to some addiction specialists, another way to increase participation in substance abuse programs is to change the public's attitude about addiction. "Addiction remains a disease of guilt and shame, and there are a lot of people who look down their noses at people who suffer from the disease," said Dr. Kirk Moberg of the Illinois Institute for Addiction Recovery. "We need to change our whole philosophy and culture so that addiction is looked at like high blood pressure, or diabetes, or even cancer. And I mention cancer because addiction kills just like cancer does."[10] Destigmatizing addiction may make people more willing to admit they need help.

Alternative pain management techniques, such as yoga, offer some people pain relief without the need for medication.

ALTERNATIVE PAIN MANAGEMENT

Because many addictions begin with a legitimate prescription, in 2016, the CDC released new prescribing guidelines for the use of opioids for chronic pain. The guidelines recommend low dosages and continual risk assessment to determine whether a patient is in danger of developing an addiction. Although the CDC guidelines are only recommendations, not laws, some states have gone further. New Jersey, for example, has restricted first-time opioid prescriptions to five days. Some insurance companies and pharmacies have also become involved, refusing to fill new opioid prescriptions of more than seven to ten days.

Some health-care providers are also experimenting with alternative pain management techniques including massage, acupuncture, physical therapy, and yoga. Alternate pain treatments often involve not only the body but also the mind, through counseling, mindfulness training, hypnosis, and other therapies. According to David Shurtleff, of the National Center for Complementary and Integrative Health, "We now understand that pain is not just a sensation but a brain state. And mind-body interventions may be particularly helpful."[11]

NEW PAIN MEDICATIONS

Even as some health-care providers look for alternative ways to treat pain, pharmaceutical companies are working to develop abuse-deterrent formulations (ADFs) of opioid medications. These drugs contain the same opioids as other pain relievers but cannot be snorted or injected. Several ADF opioids are already available, and pharmaceutical companies are also working to develop abuse-deterrent stimulants. ADFs often come in the form of

GOOD SAMARITANS

Immediate access to emergency care is critical in an overdose. Yet in some cases, people witnessing an overdose are afraid to call for help out of fear they will be prosecuted for drug possession. In order to encourage more people to call for emergency help, most states have expanded their Good Samaritan laws. These laws protect both the person making the call and the victim of the overdose from arrest or prosecution for possession of certain drugs at the time of the emergency. The term *Good Samaritan* refers to a story in the Bible. It tells of a man who aided a traveler from the region of Samaria who had been beaten and robbed. The men were from different religious and cultural backgrounds.

capsules that are difficult to crush and are filled with a gel too thick to be injected.

Beyond reformulating current drugs, pharmaceutical companies are working to develop new, nonaddictive medications for pain and other disorders. Such alternative medications may involve substances known as biased agonists, which activate only the pain-relief branch of opioid receptors without providing side effects such as euphoria or respiratory depression. Other, nonopioid pain treatment options may someday include cannabinoids, gene therapy, or brain stimulation technologies. Cannabinoids are compounds found in marijuana, and gene therapy involves delivering nucleic acid into a person's cells to medically treat a disease. Brain stimulation is a procedure that utilizes electrical impulses to stimulate the brain.

Unused prescription drugs can be disposed of at drug take-back events or by taking them out of the container and mixing them with used coffee grounds, dirt, or cat litter and then placing them in a sealed bag in the trash.

OVERCOMING THE CRISIS

Whatever the future of pain-relief technology, one thing has become clear: something must be done to stem the prescription drug epidemic in the United States. "A truly massive response, much larger than we have had so far, is immediately necessary at all levels of society and government," says Dr. Michael Lyons of the University of Cincinnati College of Medicine. "For the most part, our country simply has not come to terms with how large and how difficult this problem is. This problem should never have happened at this scale. Now that it has, we are tragically behind in fixing it."[12] Other experts agree, saying that the death rate from overdoses is likely to climb higher until new approaches to ending the epidemic are put into action.

But others are more optimistic about the potential to end the epidemic. Kana Enomoto of SAMHSA emphasizes that "substance misuse and addiction are solvable problems." But she stresses that "the addiction problem touches us all. We all need to play a part in solving it."[13] That happens when young people choose to say no to nonmedical use of prescription drugs, when family members help their loved ones get treatment for substance use disorders, and when doctors, the government, and other entities work together to develop new ways to treat medical disorders.

VIRTUAL REALITY FOR PAIN

Some doctors are trying a unique treatment to help reduce patients' pain: virtual reality (VR). Patients are given virtual reality games to play during painful treatments or after surgery. They wear a headset and headphones to experience a computer-generated environment. In one study, patients reported a 53 percent reduction in pain after virtual reality.[14] New studies have shown the potential for VR to alleviate chronic pain as well. Doctors believe virtual reality is able to relieve pain because it distracts the brain from focusing on pain signals.

ESSENTIAL FACTS

EFFECTS ON THE BODY

- Opioids: pain relief, euphoria, numbness, drowsiness, confusion, dizziness, nausea, slowed breathing and heart rate, addiction

- Stimulants: increased feelings of alertness and energy, pleasure, increased heart rate and respiration, headache, nausea, dizziness, nervousness, inability to sleep, addiction

- Depressants: feelings of drowsiness and calm, slurred speech, shallow breathing, sleepiness, disorientation, headache, light-headedness, loss of coordination, slowed heart rate and respiration, addiction

LAWS AND POLICIES

- Prescription drugs are governed by the Controlled Substances Act. They fall into Schedules II through V of the act, depending on their potential for abuse. Morphine and hydrocodone are Schedule II drugs with high potential for abuse, while cough medications containing codeine are Schedule IV drugs. In 2016, the CDC released new guidelines recommending only short-term prescriptions for opioid pain relievers used for acute pain. Taking a medicine prescribed for another person is illegal.

IMPACT ON SOCIETY

- Prescription medications are used to cure a variety of both physical and mental ailments. Yet their abuse leads to nearly 30,000 deaths a year. Abuse of prescription drugs also costs the nation billions of dollars a year in health-care costs, lost productivity, criminal justice expenses, and foster care. An increase in injected opioids has fueled a rise in cases of HIV and hepatitis C. In the workplace, businesses may have trouble finding workers who can pass a drug test. Prescription drugs tear families apart, as parents can overdose on opioids and other drugs, leaving children behind to be raised by a grandparent or the foster care system.

QUOTE

"We can label drugs as being 'good' or 'bad,' medicinal or illicit. However, the body doesn't care about the name of the drug or from where the drug came. The body, and more specifically the targets [of the drug], react according to the chemistry of the drugs."

—*Nicole Kwiek, director of undergraduate studies, Ohio State University College of Pharmacy*

ACUPUNCTURE

The practice of using needles to pierce specific parts of the body for the purpose of pain relief or disease treatment.

AGONIST

A drug or natural body chemical that binds to a receptor to activate it.

ANTAGONIST

A drug or natural body chemical that binds to a receptor but does not activate it, blocking or reversing the action of another substance.

BLACK MARKET

A collection of buyers and sellers trading illegally.

BRAIN STIMULATION

Medical treatment that involves stimulating specific areas of the brain with electricity.

CANNABINOIDS

Chemical substances found in the cannabis plant, or marijuana.

CENTRAL NERVOUS SYSTEM

The brain and spinal cord, which transmit sensory and motor impulses through the body.

CHRONIC

Continuing for a long time.

GENE THERAPY

The process of replacing defective genes with genetically altered genes to treat a disorder or fight a disease.

LOZENGE

A small medicinal tablet usually used to treat sore throats.

LSD

Lysergic acid diethylamide, a Schedule I drug that causes powerful hallucinations.

METHAMPHETAMINE

A Schedule II drug derived from amphetamine but with more powerful stimulating effects than amphetamine.

MORAL

Having to do with ideas of right and wrong.

PAPYRUS

A material prepared in ancient Egypt from a water plant, used in writing.

PARALEGAL

A person who is trained in legal matters to assist attorneys.

PSILOCYBIN

A hallucinogenic drug derived from mushrooms.

RELAPSE

To fall or slip back into a former practice.

SUMERIAN

From Sumer, an ancient civilization established in Mesopotamia in the fourth century BCE.

TINCTURE

A solution of a medicinal substance in alcohol or alcohol and water.

ADDITIONAL RESOURCES

SELECTED BIBLIOGRAPHY

Gahlinger, Paul. *Illegal Drugs: A Complete Guide to Their History, Chemistry, Use, and Abuse*. New York: Penguin, 2004. Print.

Jones, Keith, ed. *Drug Abuse Sourcebook*. Detroit, MI: Omnigraphics, 2016. Print.

Newton, David E. *Prescription Drug Abuse*. Santa Barbara, CA: ABC-CLIO, 2016. Print.

FURTHER READINGS

Abramowitz, Melissa. *Heroin and Prescription Opioids*. Minneapolis: Abdo, 2019. Print.

Bodden, Valerie. *Club and Prescription Drug Abuse*. Minneapolis: Abdo, 2015. Print.

Gillar, Arthur, ed. *Drug Abuse*. Detroit, MI: Greenhaven, 2013. Print.

ONLINE RESOURCES

Booklinks
NONFICTION NETWORK
FREE! ONLINE NONFICTION RESOURCES

To learn more about prescription and over-the-counter drugs, visit **abdobooklinks.com.** These links are routinely monitored and updated to provide the most current information available.

MORE INFORMATION

For more information on this subject, contact or visit the
following organizations:

DAVID J. SENCER CDC MUSEUM

1600 Clifton Road NE
Atlanta, GA 30329
404-639-0830
cdc.gov/museum/index.htm

This free museum presents exhibits that highlight public health issues. Each
summer, high school juniors and seniors can attend Disease Detective Camp to
explore the field of public health.

DEA MUSEUM

700 Army Navy Drive
Arlington, VA 22202
202-307-3463
deamuseum.org

Offering free admission, the DEA Museum seeks to educate the public on the
history of drugs, addiction, and drug law enforcement in the United States.

NATIONAL INSTITUTE ON DRUG ABUSE

6001 Executive Boulevard
Bethesda, MD 20892
301-443-1124
drugabuse.gov

The National Institute on Drug Abuse is a government organization dedicated
to advancing the science of drug use and addiction to improve public health.

CHAPTER 1. A NATIONAL EPIDEMIC

1. "Overdose Death Rates." *National Institute on Drug Abuse.* National Institute on Drug Abuse, Sept. 2017. Web. 15 Mar. 2018.

2. *Unprescribed: Prescription for Addiction.* Holland, OH: Dreamscape, 2014. DVD.

3. "National Study: Teen Misuse and Abuse of Prescription Drugs Up 33 Percent Since 2008, Stimulants Contributing to Sustained Rx Epidemic." *Partnership for Drug-Free Kids.* Partnership for Drug-Free Kids, 22 Apr. 2013. Web. 15 Mar. 2018.

4. Julie Turkewitz. "'The Pills Are Everywhere': How the Opioid Crisis Claims Its Youngest Victims." *New York Times.* New York Times, 20 Sept. 2017. Web. 1 Oct. 2017.

5. Turkewitz, "'The Pills Are Everywhere.'"

6. Kate Miller. "The Last All-Nighter." *New York Times.* New York Times, 4 Mar. 2013. Web. 1 Oct. 2017.

7. Paul Gahlinger. *Illegal Drugs: A Complete Guide to Their History, Chemistry, Use, and Abuse.* New York: Penguin, 2004. Print. 9.

8. Nicole Kwiek. "Chemical Structures of 'Good' and 'Bad' Drugs Dictate Functions." *Generation Rx.* The Ohio State University College of Pharmacy, 3 July 2015. Web. 1 Oct. 2017.

9. Nadia Kounang. "Opioid Overdoses Shorten US Life Expectancy by 2 ½ Months." *CNN.* CNN, 19 Sept. 2017. Web. 1 Oct. 2017.

CHAPTER 2. USE AND ABUSE

1. Paul Gahlinger. *Illegal Drugs: A Complete Guide to Their History, Chemistry, Use, and Abuse.* New York: Penguin, 2004. Print. 19–20.

2. Kenneth Pletcher. "Opium Wars." *Encyclopedia Britannica.* Encyclopedia Britannica, n.d. Web. 15 Mar. 2017.

3. Gahlinger, *Illegal Drugs,* 29, 58.

4. "Heroin, Morphine and Opiates." *History.* A+E Television Networks, n.d. Web. 1 Dec. 2017.

5. *Unprescribed: Prescription for Addiction.* Holland, OH: Dreamscape, 2014. DVD.

6. Gahlinger, *Illegal Drugs,* 29, 58.

7. Gahlinger, *Illegal Drugs,* 5.

CHAPTER 3. DRUG CULTURE

1. David E. Newton. *Prescription Drug Abuse.* Santa Barbara, CA: ABC-CLIO, 2016. Print. 141.

2. Dina Gusovsky. "Americans Consume Vast Majority of the World's Opioids." *CNBC.* CNBC, 27 Apr. 2016. Web. 1 Dec. 2017.

3. Newton, *Prescription Drug Abuse,* 160.

4. "America's Behavioral Health Changes and Challenges." *Key Substance Use and Mental Health Indicators in the United States: Results from the 2016 National Survey on Drug Use and Health. SAMHSA.* SAMHSA, n.d. Web. 1 Oct. 2017.

5. "America's Behavioral Health Changes and Challenges."

6. Richard Pérez-Peña. "Ohio Sues Drug Makers, Saying They Aided Opioid Epidemic." *New York Times.* New York Times, 31 May 2017. Web. 1 Oct. 2017.

7. "America's Behavioral Health Changes and Challenges."

8. "America's Behavioral Health Changes and Challenges."

9. Josh Katz. "Drug Deaths in America Are Rising Faster Than Ever." *New York Times.* New York Times, 5 June 2017. Web. 1 Oct. 2017.

10. "Detailed Tables." *Key Substance Use and Mental Health Indicators in the United States: Results from the 2016 National Survey on Drug Use and Health. SAMHSA.* SAMHSA, 2016. Web. 1 Oct. 2017.

11. "Detailed Tables."

12. Nadia Kounang. "Opioid Overdoses Shorten US Life Expectancy by 2 ½ Months." *CNN*. CNN, 19 Sept. 2017. Web. 15 Mar. 2018.

13. "Monitoring the Future 2016 Survey Results." *National Institute on Drug Abuse*. National Institute on Drug Abuse, 2016. Web. 1 Oct. 2017.

14. Katz, "Drug Deaths in America Are Rising Faster Than Ever."

15. "Detailed Tables."

16. "Chasing the Dragon: The Life of an Opiate Addict." *Just Think Twice*. Drug Enforcement Administration, 5 Feb. 2016. Web. 1 Dec. 2017.

17. "The Partnership Attitude Tracking Study." *Partnership for Drug Free Kids*. Partnership for Drug Free Kids, 2013. Web. 1 Dec. 2017.

18. Cindy Mogil. *Swallowing a Bitter Pill*. Far Hills, NJ: New Horizons, 2001. Print. 122.

19. "Chasing the Dragon."

20. "Chasing the Dragon."

21. "Chasing the Dragon."

CHAPTER 4. OPIOIDS

1. "Opioid Overdose." *CDC*. US Department of Health & Human Services, n.d. Web. 23 Oct. 2017.

2. *Drug Abuse Sourcebook*. Detroit: Omnigraphics, 2016. Print. 80.

3. Haley Sweetland Edwards. "The Drug Cascade." *Time*. 3 July 2017. *Ebsco Masterfile Premier*.

4. Dennis Thompson. "More than 1 in 3 Americans Prescribed Opioids." *CBS News*. CBS Interactive, 1 Aug. 2017. Web. 1 Dec. 2017.

5. Gregg Easterbrook. "Painkillers, NFL's Other Big Problem." *ESPN*. ESPN, 26 May 2014. Web. 1 Dec. 2017.

6. Nadia Kounang. "Lawsuit Alleges that NFL Teams Gave Painkillers Recklessly." *CNN*. CNN, 13 Mar. 2017. Web. 15 Mar. 2018.

7. Jennifer Morlan. "Opioid Crisis: 'You Know Someone Who Is Affected by This." *IndyStar*. USA Today, 1 Oct. 2017. Web. 1 Dec. 2017.

8. "Detailed Tables." *Key Substance Use and Mental Health Indicators in the United States: Results from the 2016 National Survey on Drug Use and Health. SAMHSA*. SAMHSA, 2016. Web. 1 Oct. 2017.

9. David E. Newton. *Prescription Drug Abuse*. Santa Barbara, CA: ABC-CLIO, 2016. Print. 99.

10. "Prescription Opioids and Heroin: Prescription Opioid Abuse Is a Risk Factor for Heroin Use." *National Institute on Drug Abuse*. National Institute on Drug Abuse, Dec. 2015. Web. 1 Dec. 2017.

11. "Chasing the Dragon: The Life of an Opiate Addict." *Just Think Twice*. Drug Enforcement Administration, 5 Feb. 2016. Web. 1 Dec. 2017.

12. "Overdose Death Rates." *National Institute on Drug Abuse*. National Institute on Drug Abuse, Sept. 2017. Web. 15 Mar. 2018.

13. John Keilman. "As More Heroin Is Mixed with Fentanyl, Opioid Crisis Turns Even Deadlier." *Chicago Tribune*. Chicago Tribune, 28 Aug. 2017. Web. 1 Dec. 2017.

14. Thomas Catan and Evan Perez. "A Pain-Drug Champion Has Second Thoughts." *Wall Street Journal*. Wall Street Journal, 17 Dec. 2012. Web. 1 Nov. 2017.

CHAPTER 5. STIMULANTS

1. Kevin Loria. "Some Competitive Video Gamers Are Abusing Drugs to Get an Edge." *Business Insider*. Business Insider, 15 Jan. 2016. Web. 1 Dec. 2017.

2. Richard A. Friedman. "Why Are We Drugging Our Soldiers?" *New York Times*. New York Times, 21 Apr. 2012. Web. 1 Dec. 2017.

SOURCE NOTES CONTINUED

CHAPTER 6. DEPRESSANTS

1. Cesar Gamboa. "Nearly 92 Million Adults Used Prescription Opioids, New Gov't Report." *Addiction Now*. Addiction Now, 21 Aug. 2017. Web. 1 Dec. 2017.

2. "The Truth about Prescription Drug Abuse." *Foundation for a Drug-Free World*. Foundation for a Drug-Free World, 2015. Web. 1 Nov. 2017.

3. "Overdose Death Rates." *National Institute on Drug Abuse*. National Institute on Drug Abuse, Sept. 2017. Web. 1 Dec. 2017.

4. Paul Gahlinger. *Illegal Drugs: A Complete Guide to Their History, Chemistry, Use, and Abuse*. New York: Penguin, 2004. Print. 225.

5. "The Truth About Prescription Drug Abuse."

CHAPTER 7. OVER-THE-COUNTER DRUGS

1. "Top Ten OTC Medicines and Herbals Abused by Teens and Young Adults." *Consumer Med Safety*. Consumer Med Safety, 5 Oct. 2014. Web. 1 Nov. 2017.

2. "The Truth About Prescription Drug Abuse." *Foundation for a Drug-Free World*. Foundation for a Drug-Free World, 2015. Web. 1 Nov. 2017.

3. Mary Elizabeth May. "Dextromethorphan." *National Capital Poison Center*. National Capital Poison Center, n.d. Web. 12 Apr. 2018.

CHAPTER 8. ADDICTION AND TREATMENT

1. "Substance Use Disorder." *SAMHSA*. SAMHSA, 27 Oct. 2015. Web.

2. "Detailed Tables." *Key Substance Use and Mental Health Indicators in the United States: Results from the 2016 National Survey on Drug Use and Health*. *SAMHSA*. SAMHSA, 2016. Web. 1 Oct. 2017.

3. "Detailed Tables."

4. "Definition of Addiction." *American Society of Addiction Medicine*. American Society of Addiction Medicine, 19 Apr. 2011. Web. 1 Nov. 2017.

5. Mitchell Byars. "'The Image of an Addict Has Changed': Behind Boulder County's Opioid Crisis." *The Daily Camera*. Digital First Media, 7 Oct. 2017. Web. 1 Nov. 2017.

6. Erin Marie Daly. *Generation Rx: A Story of Dope, Death, and America's Opiate Crisis*. Berkeley, CA: Counterpoint, 2014. Print. 15.

7. "Chasing the Dragon: The Life of an Opiate Addict." *Just Think Twice*. Drug Enforcement Administration, 5 Feb. 2016. Web. 1 Dec. 2017.

8. Elizabeth Flock. "How Treating Opioids with More Opioids Has Divided the Recovery Community." *PBS NewsHour*. PBS, 5 Oct. 2017. Web. 1 Nov. 2017.

9. "Medication-Assisted Treatment for Opioid Addiction." *Partnership for Drug-Free Kids*. Partnership for Drug-Free Kids, n.d. Web. 1 Nov. 2017.

10. "Risks for Relapse, Overdose, and What You Can Do." *Partnership for Drug-Free Kids*. Partnership for Drug-Free Kids, n.d. Web. 1 Nov. 2017.

CHAPTER 9. IMPACT ON SOCIETY

1. "Trends & Statistics." *National Institute on Drug Abuse*. National Institute on Drug Abuse, Apr. 2017. Web. 1 Nov. 2017.

2. "How Does Drug Abuse Affect Society and You?" *Drug Rehab*. Drug Rehab, 2 Jan. 2015. Web. 1 Nov. 2017.

3. "Families in Crisis: The Human Service Implications of Rural Opioid Misuse." *National Advisory Committee on Rural Health and Human Services*. HRSA.gov, July 2016. Web. 1 Nov. 2017.

4. Bruc Schackman, et al. "The Lifetime Medical Cost Savings from Preventing HIV in the United States." *Med Care*. Med Care, Apr. 2015. Web. 1 Nov. 2017.

5. Sheelah Kolhatkar. "The Cost of the Opioid Crisis." *New Yorker*. New Yorker, 18 Sept. 2017. Web. 1 Dec. 2017.

6. Lynne Curry. "How the Opioid Crisis Could Affect Your Workplace." *Alaska Daily News*. Anchorage Daily News, 28 Aug. 2017. 1 Nov. 2017.

7. "How the Opioid Crisis Decimated the American Workforce." *PBS New Hour*. PBS, 5 Oct. 2017. Web. 1 Nov. 2017.

8. Kolhatkar, "The Cost of the Opioid Crisis."

9. Steven Reinberg. "Significant Spike in Opioid-Related Car Crash Deaths." *CBS News*. CBS News, 31 July 2017. Web. 1 Nov. 2017.

10. John Caniglia. "Cost of Opioid Epidemic Soars, Hitting Taxpayers Harder Than Ever." *Cleveland.com*. Advance Ohio, 8 Oct. 2017. Web. 1 Nov. 2017.

11. Julia Lurie. "Children of the Opioid Epidemic Are Flooding Foster Homes." *Mother Jones*. Mother Jones, July/Aug. 2017. Web. 1 Nov. 2017.

12. Deborah Feyerick. "A Generation of Heroin Orphans." *CNN*. CNN, 1 May 2017. Web. 1 Dec. 2017.

13. "How Does Drug Abuse Affect Society and You?"

14. "How Does Drug Abuse Affect Society and You?"

15. Drug Enforcement Administration. "Counterfeit Prescription Pills Containing Fentanyl: A Global Threat." *DEA Intelligence Brief*. DEA, July 2016. Web. 1 Nov. 2017.

16. Christian Nordqvist. "Prescription Drugs Linked to Most Fatal Overdoses." *Medical News Today*. Healthline Media UK, 20 Feb. 2013. Web. 1 Dec. 2017.

CHAPTER 10. FIGHTING THE CRISIS

1. "Trump to Soon Declare National Emergency Over Opioid Epidemic." *CNN*. CNN, 19 Oct. 2017. Web. 1 Dec. 2017.

2. Dan Merica. "What Trump's Opioid Announcement Means—and Doesn't Mean." *CNN*. CNN, 26 Oct. 2017. Web. 1 Dec. 2017.

3. Stephani Sutherlani. "Rethinking Relief." *Scientific American Mind*. May/June 2017. Web. *Ebsco Masterfile Premier*.

4. Thomas Catan and Evan Perez. "A Pain-Drug Champion Has Second Thoughts." *Wall Street Journal*. Wall Street Journal, 17 Dec. 2012. Web. 1 Dec. 2017.

5. Christopher Zara. "Treated Like Addicts." *Vice News*. Vice Media, 24 Oct. 2016. Web. 1 Dec. 2017.

6. Merica, "What Trump's Opioid Announcement Means."

7. Elizabeth Foy Larsen. "Good Teens Turned Drug Addicts." *Scholastic Choices*. Oct. 2014. Web. *Ebsco MasterFile Premier*.

8. David E. Newton. *Prescription Drug Abuse*. Santa Barbara, CA: ABC-CLIO, 2016. Print. 134.

9. "Drug Overdose Death Data." *Centers for Disease Control and Prevention*. CDC, 16 Dec. 2016. Web.1 Dec. 2017.

10. "Special Report: Smart Drugs." *25 News Week.com*. Week Television, n.d. Web. 1 Dec. 2017.

11. Sutherlani, "Rethinking Relief."

12. Korin Miller. "Drug Overdoses May Now Be the Leading Cause of Death for Young People." *Self*. Condé Nast, 7 June 2017. Web. 1 Dec. 2017.

13. *Facing Addiction in America: The Surgeon General's Report on Alcohol, Drugs, and Health*. Washington DC: US Department of Health and Human Services, Nov. 2016. Web. 1 Nov. 2017.

14. Christina Loguidice. "Virtual Reality for Pain Management: A Weapon Against the Opioid Epidemic?" *Clinical Pain Advisor*. Clinical Pain Advisor, 5 Sept. 2017. Web. 1 Nov. 2017.

INDEX

Valerie Bodden is the author of more than 250 nonfiction children's books. Her books have received critical acclaim from *School Library Journal, Booklist, Children's Literature, ForeWord Magazine, Horn Book Guide, VOYA,* and *Library Media Connection*. Valerie lives in Wisconsin with her husband, four children, one dog, two cats, a growing collection of fish, and miscellaneous bugs that her children have "rescued" from the outdoors.